DISCOVERY & EXPLORATION

Exploring North America, 1800–1900

Revised Edition

DISCOVERY & EXPLORATION

Exploration in the World of the Ancients,
    Revised Edition

Exploration in the World of the Middle Ages,
    500–1500, Revised Edition

Exploration in the Age of Empire, 1750–1953,
    Revised Edition

Exploring the Pacific, Revised Edition

Exploring the Polar Regions, Revised Edition

Discovery of the Americas, 1492–1800,
    Revised Edition

Opening Up North America, 1497–1800,
    Revised Edition

Across America: The Lewis and Clark Expedition,
    Revised Edition

Exploring North America, 1800–1900, Revised Edition

Exploring Space, Revised Edition

Exploring North America, 1800–1900

Revised Edition

MAURICE ISSERMAN

JOHN S. BOWMAN and MAURICE ISSERMAN
General Editors

CHELSEA HOUSE
PUBLISHERS
An imprint of Infobase Publishing

Chelsea House
An imprint of Infobase Publishing
132 West 31st Street
New York, NY 10001

Library of Congress Cataloging-in-Publication Data
Isserman, Maurice.
  Exploring North America, 1800-1900 / Maurice Isserman ; John S. Bowman and Maurice Isserman, general editors. -- Rev. ed.
      p. cm. -- (Discovery and exploration)
  Includes bibliographical references and index.
  ISBN 978-1-60413-194-9 (hardcover)
  1. North America--Discovery and exploration--Juvenile literature. 2. Explorers --North America--History--19th century--Juvenile literature. 3. North America--History--19th century--Juvenile literature. I. Bowman, John Stewart, 1931- II. Title.
  E45.I85 2010
  970.01--dc22   2009027860

Chelsea House books are available at special discounts when purchased in bulk quantities for businesses, associations, institutions, or sales promotions. Please call our Special Sales Department in New York at (212) 967-8800 or (800) 322-87

You can find Chelsea House on the World Wide Web at
http://www.chelseahouse.com

Text design by Erika K. Arroyo
Cover design by Alicia Post
Composition by EJB Publishing Services
Cover printed by Bang Printing, Brainerd, MN
Book printed and bound by Bang Printing, Brainerd, MN
Date printed: December 2009
Printed in the United States of America

10 9 8 7 6 5 4 3 2 1

Contents

1 DOWN THE "GREAT UNKNOWN"—
GRAND CANYON, SUMMER 1869   7

2 THOMAS JEFFERSON'S OTHER EXPLORERS   22

3 FUR TRADERS AND THE EXPLORATION
OF THE WESTERN FRONTIER   42

4 THE EXPLORATION OF WESTERN CANADA   59

5 THE U.S. ARMY CORPS OF TOPOGRAPHICAL
ENGINEERS   72

6 JOHN C. FRÉMONT AND THE EXPLORATION
OF CALIFORNIA   84

7 NATURAL HISTORY, ART, AND SCIENCE   100

8 THE EXPLORATION OF ALASKA   114

9 WILDERNESS PRESERVATION   125

Chronology and Timeline   134

Glossary   138

Bibliography   140

Further Resources   142

Picture Credits   144

Index   145

About the Contributors   151

1

Down the "Great Unknown"
Grand Canyon, Summer 1869

ON THE MORNING OF AUGUST 13, 1869, JOHN WESLEY POWELL AND the men of the Colorado River Exploring Expedition sat by the water's edge, contemplating the rapids they were about to attempt in their battered wooden boats. On either side of the river the walls of the Grand Canyon rose to a dizzying three-quarters of a mile above their heads. At the top of the canyon, spreading out for miles as far as the eyes could see, lay arid deserts. They had come across few signs of humans in weeks. Powell and his men wondered if they would live to see another day.

In his 35 years, Powell had known more than his share of danger and adversity, and he tried not to show his misgivings that day. The men called him "Major" in honor of his service in the Union Army in the Civil War, when he had lost an arm in combat. But on this August morning, John Wesley Powell felt he was facing the supreme challenge of his life.

THE GREAT UNKNOWN

"We are now ready to start on our way down the Great Unknown," John Wesley Powell recalled. "Our boats, tied to a common stake, are chafing each other, as they are tossed by the fretful river. They ride high and buoyant, for their loads are lighter than we could desire. We have but a month's rations remaining."

Powell and his men had started their journey down the Colorado less than three months before. When they began, they had a 10-month supply of food. They had lost most of the food to the rough river. They had managed to save a little of their flour, which they dried and sifted

7

Although geologist and explorer John Wesley Powell led several expeditions into the Rocky Mountains, he is most famous for the 1869 expedition where he sailed down the Colorado and Green rivers, making the first passage through the Grand Canyon.

through mosquito netting. This took out the lumps. They had a little bacon and a few pounds of dried apples. Their only luxury was a large sack of coffee. Despite this, Powell tried to look on the bright side. "The lightening of the boats has this advantage; they will ride the waves better, and we shall have but little to carry when we make a portage."

The men expected the trip to be hard and could put up with little food. It was the unknown that bothered them. "We have an unknown distance yet to run; an unknown river yet to explore," Powell wrote. "What falls there are, we know not; what rocks beset the channel, we know not; what walls rise over the river, we know not." There was no turning back. All they could do was push the boats out once again into the river's current and see where it would carry them.

Powell's men may have called him "Major," but he and they were not soldiers. Unlike Meriwether Lewis and William Clark, who were under orders from President Thomas Jefferson, Powell followed no orders but his own. His men took orders from him only as long as they chose to do so. Powell and his men were not hoping to get rich, like the fur-hunting mountain men who followed Lewis and Clark up the Missouri and across the Continental Divide. Nobody's fortune would be made by going down the Colorado in 1869; this was a scientific enterprise. It was funded by universities and museums, with a little help from the federal government in the form of military rations. They were also loaned some scientific instruments from the Smithsonian Institution in Washington, D.C.

Powell's men were on this journey for a number of reasons, including a love of adventure. Perhaps they also hoped to win some measure of glory and fame. Nonetheless, the main goal of the expedition was knowledge, for its own sake. If they were successful, Powell and his men would fill in a blank space on the map of the American West—the course of the Colorado River as it wound its way through the desert country of northern Arizona.

THE COLORADO RIVER

The Colorado River is one of five great rivers that begin in the southern Rocky Mountains. The Rockies are a chain of mountain ranges that extend from northern Mexico to northern Canada. The Rockies' peaks range from 7,000 feet (2,133 meters) to 14,000 feet (4,267 m). The Continental Divide runs among the peaks of the southern Rockies. Three rivers—the Arkansas, the South Platte, and the North Platte—drain to the east of the southern Rockies. One, the Rio Grande, drains to the south. The Colorado drains to the west.

The Colorado's headwaters are found in Grand Lake on the Rockies' western slope, at an altitude of 8,369 feet (2,550 m). Today, it is part of Rocky Mountain National Park in northern Colorado. From there, the Colorado flows southwest through Utah, into northern Arizona and the southeastern corner of Nevada. Then it swings nearly due south and flows into Mexico. It finally empties its waters into the Gulf of California.

At 1,440 miles (2,317 kilometers), the Colorado is the fifth longest river in the United States and drains nearly 250,000 square miles (402,336 sq km) of land. Its tributary rivers and streams make up the chief river system of the American Southwest. Among those tributaries is the Green River, flowing south from the Wind River Range in Wyoming, the river that Powell and his men took to reach the Colorado. For millions of years it cut deeply through the layers of stone that make up the Colorado Plateau. In the process, it produced one of the most spectacular canyons and gorges to be found in North America. The most spectacular of all is the Grand Canyon, which stretches for 277 miles (365 km). In some places its bottom lies a mile below Earth's surface.

The banks of the Colorado had been home to Native American tribes for centuries, long before the first Europeans stumbled upon it. In 1539, Spanish explorer Francisco de Ulloa discovered its mouth on the Gulf of California. Another Spaniard, Hernando de Alarcón, sailed a short way up the river in 1540, calling it El Río de Buena Guia, or the River of Good Guidance. It would later be renamed Colorado (or colored) for the reddish silt carried by its waters. García López de Cárdenas, an officer attached to the well-known Spanish explorer Francisco Vásquez de Coronado's expedition, came upon the Grand Canyon in 1540. He was traveling overland and was absolutely astonished to find this deeply cut fissure in the desert. Cárdenas and his men, however, never set foot on the floor of the canyon they discovered, for the prospect of descending its steep walls to the river proved far too daunting.

The deserts surrounding the Grand Canyon were not welcoming lands. For the next three centuries Spanish explorers, missionaries, and soldiers rarely visited the region. When the United States acquired the territory in the Treaty of Guadalupe Hidalgo, which ended the Mexican War in 1848, the nearest sizable white settlements were hundreds of miles away. No European had ever attempted to travel the length of the Colorado River as it runs its westward course through the Grand Canyon. That is, until John Wesley Powell and the men of the Colorado River Exploring Expedition.

THE EXPEDITION BEGINS

John Wesley Powell and his team began their journey on May 11, 1869, at Green River Station in the Wyoming Territory. This was a stop on the newly opened Union Pacific railroad line. They spent two weeks in Green River packing their supplies. There were 10 of them altogether in the expeditionary party. In addition to Powell was his brother, Walter, another veteran of the Union Army, and two other brothers, Oramel and Seneca Howland. The Howlands had been with the Powells on an earlier Colorado Rockies expedition. Hunters Bill Dunn and Jack Sumner and cook Billy Rhodes Hawkins were also veterans of the previous expedition. There were also some new recruits, including an 18-year-old ox driver named Andrew "Dare Devil Dick" Hall, an expert boatsman and army veteran named George Young Bradley, and an adventure-seeking Englishman named Frank Goodman.

To carry them downriver, they had four boats that Powell had ordered built in Chicago and shipped by rail to Green River. Three were made of oak, 21 feet (6.4 m) long, and steered by a wooden sweep from the stern. They had watertight compartments built within at either end to hold the expedition supplies. These heavy boats were designed to stand up to the beating they would take from the river rapids. The men named the three boats *Maid of the Canyon*, *Kitty Clyde's Sister*, and the *No-Name*. The fourth boat was smaller and lighter, just 16 feet (4.8 m) long, and built of pine. Lighter and easier to steer, it would be Powell's pilot boat, guiding the heavier-laden craft that followed. Powell named it the *Emma Dean*, after his wife.

The rations they packed in Green River included bacon, beans, flour, sugar, coffee, clothing, guns and ammunition, blankets, and tents. They had carpentry tools in case the boats needed repair and also to build cabins along the river's banks. There were also scientific instruments, including two sextants, four chronometers, barometers, thermometers, and compasses. Powell planned to map the river's every twist and turn.

On May 24, 1869, they pushed their boats into the Green River. "The good people of Green River City turn out to see us start," Powell would later write. The crowd, some doubting they would ever see the explorers alive again, cheered the men in the boats. "We raise our little flag, push the boats from shore, and the swift current carries us down."

The first day's cruise was a foreshadowing of troubles to come. They had not made it a mile from their launching point when the boats ran onto a sandbar and had to be partially unloaded before they would float free. An oar broke against a rock, and two other oars were lost in the current, though eventually recovered. Yet, the pleasure of being on their way at last and the views in the distance rewarded the men for their hard work.

For two days the Green River carried them due south through open land. On May 26, they had traveled 62 miles (99 km) from the starting point. Entering higher ground, the river cut a passage through the Uinta Mountains. They halted for a few days at the entrance of the canyon, which they called Flaming Gorge for the red sandstone walls that rose 1,200 feet (365 m) to either side of the river. On May 29, Powell climbed to the clifftop (he proved a remarkably adept rock climber, given that he had only one arm). From there he looked back over the route they had traveled down to the canyon's mouth. He could see a dwelling in the distance, which he knew to be the home of a white rancher. It made him think of the history of the region over the past few decades:

> For many years, this valley has been the home of a number of mountaineers, who were originally hunters and trappers, living with the Indians. Most of them have one or more Indian wives. They no longer roam with the nomadic tribes in pursuit of buckskin or beaver, but have accumulated herds of cattle and horses, and consider themselves quite well-to-do.

Pushing on, they passed through Horseshoe Canyon (which they named for its curving shape) and Kingfisher Canyon (named for the birds that fished its streams). At another turn in the river, they came upon a dome-shaped rocky point whose surface had been pitted by erosion. Swallows had nested in the pits, and as they flew around the cliffs, they looked to Powell like "swarm[s] of bees"—which led to the name Beehive Point. On May 31, the expedition reached the mouth of Red Canyon. There the men found evidence that they were not the first white men to sail this far down the Green River. On the canyon wall were painted the words "Ashley, 1825." Although Powell had never heard of "Ashley," the inscription was left no doubt by William H. Ashley, a pioneering fur trapper who had come in search of beaver (which by 1869 had nearly been trapped into extinction).

There were good days and bad days on the river. When the river was calm or the rapids relatively gentle, they made quick progress. But all too often they encountered dangerous stretches that forced them to stop along the shore. Then they would unload the supplies from each boat and "line" the empty boats through the danger spots. That meant attaching ropes to the bow (front of a boat) and stern (back of a boat) of each craft, then feeding out the stern line from upriver. This would allow them to ease the boat down through the most dangerous passages and pull the boat to shore again with the bow line, which had been secured farther downriver. Then they would have to carry the supplies along the shore to the boats and reload them, until the next dangerous rapids or falls came along. Then the whole process was repeated.

On June 4, Powell's little fleet reached Brown's Hole, a valley named for Baptiste Brown. Brown was a Hudson's Bay fur trader who had settled in the region in 1827. There they stayed for three days to explore. The countryside was full of vibrant signs of plant and animal life. The surrounding pine forests and grassy meadows were well watered by the melting snow of the nearby mountains. They woke to birdsong in the morning and noted the presence of warblers and woodpeckers, flickers, meadowlarks, and wild geese. Mule deer, elk, grizzly bears, wolverines, wild cats, and mountain lions could be seen or tracked in the surrounding hills. On June 5, Powell and one of his men climbed the cliffs above the river and from their height could "look up the valley of the Vermilion," through which, as he remembered, his predecessor explorer John C. Frémont "found his path on his way to the great parks of Colorado."

NEAR DISASTER

The river now swung southwest. On June 8, Powell and his team entered Lodore Canyon (the northern boundary of present-day Dinosaur National Monument). In Lodore Canyon they had an accident that nearly doomed the expedition. On June 9, the *No-Name*, manned by Frank Goodman and the Howland brothers, was sucked into the rapids as they tried to maneuver it along the shoreline. The boat hit a rock and split in two. Goodman and the Howlands were rescued, soaked and shaken, but unharmed. The boat's contents had spilled into the water, however, including much of the expedition's supply of flour, beans, and bacon. Even worse, all of the expedition's barometers had been aboard the *No-Name.* Bacon and beans could be replaced by game they shot along the river. The barometers, however, were irreplaceable. Without them, the expedition could not measure altitude and thus could not track the descent of the river from the hills toward sea level. They also could not measure the heights of the cliffs that loomed above the river. Fortunately, the next morning they found the wrecked aft section of the boat a short way downriver, washed up on a little island, and recovered from it the still-intact package of barometers.

The next few days on the river brought more near disasters. One section of rapids was so bad that they named it "Hell's Half-Mile." The *Maid of the Canyon* barely escaped the fate of the *No-Name.* Nor were they safe on shore. On June 16, a carelessly tended cooking fire ignited some dead trees around their camp. The men, "clothing burned and hair singed," as Powell later described them, had to leap into the water to escape, abandoning cookware and other provisions on shore to the flames.

On June 17, still traveling down the Green River, they reached the mouth of the Yampa River. Eleven days later they reached the mouth of the Uinta River and halted. They needed the rest. By walking 40 miles (64 km) up the Uinta River, they had their last chance of getting new supplies, at the Ute Indian reservation. Powell made the hike inland with a few of his men. At the reservation, he recalled, it was "rather pleasant to see a house once more, and some evidences of civilization, even if it is on an Indian reservation, several day's ride from the nearest home of the white man." Powell was impressed by the Utes' ability to farm in such an arid climate and by the fields of wheat, melons, and other vegetables they grew. With rainfall scarce, the Native Peoples diverted mountain streams to irrigate their crops. "Most of the crops are look-ing well," Powell wrote, "and it is rather surprising with what pride they show us that they are able to cultivate crops like white men."

On July 6, they pushed off again, now numbering nine men in three boats. The day before, Frank Goodman decided he had had enough

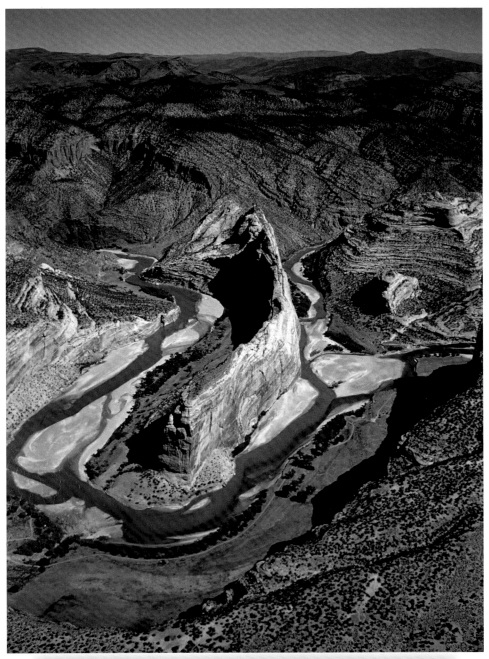

The Green River is 730 miles (1,174 km) long and winds through three states—Utah, Colorado, and Wyoming—and some of the most beautiful canyons in the United States. Above, the Green River is shown curving through the Dinosaur National Monument in Utah.

adventure after surviving the wreck of the *No-Name* and headed back east on his own.

On July 7, Powell decided to climb a cliff behind their evening camp to get a better look at the landscape. He and Bradley climbed high on the cliff, but Powell misjudged his route. He found himself on a foothold from which he could neither go forward nor retreat, with a 100-foot (30-m) drop beneath him. Clinging to a rocky knob with his one hand, he shouted to Bradley, above him on the cliff, for help. Bradley found a secure spot to sit on a ledge, took off his long underwear, and lowered the garment to Powell. Powell grabbed hold of this unlikely lifeline, and Bradley pulled him to safety.

On July 11, as they passed through landscape so bleak they named it Desolation Canyon, another near disaster befell them. Powell was thrown from the *Emma Dean* into the rapids. He was pulled from the water before drowning, but two guns and one of the precious barometers were lost.

Below Desolation Canyon, Powell's expedition ran through Coal (now Gray) Canyon, named for the gray sandstone of its walls. They spotted signs of Native American inhabitants or visitors to the canyon: rafts floating against one bank, for use in a river crossing, and arrowheads at another spot. On July 14, they came to a new canyon, which they named Labyrinth Canyon for its many twists and turns. The waters were now smoother, and the traveling grew easier. The waters grew so gentle that they named the next canyon Stillwater Canyon. Around them lay desert country: "The landscape everywhere, away from the river, is rock," Powell wrote of this stretch of their journey, "cliffs of rock; tables of rock; plateaus of rock; terraces of rock; crags of rock . . . a whole land of naked rock . . ."

Late on the afternoon of July 17, they came to the junction of the Green and the Colorado rivers, having traveled more than 500 miles (804 km) since setting out of the Green. They rested for a few days, repacked their supplies, and fixed some leaks in their boats. Undaunted by the narrowness of the escape the last time he climbed the cliffs along the river, Powell made his way up the canyon walls once again. He was rewarded with a glorious view. On July 21, they set off downriver through the turbulent waters of Cataract Canyon. Their progress slowed to as little as a mile (1.6 km) a day. The boats were leaking again, and Powell and his brother hiked up the canyon walls to gather resin from pitch pines to use for caulking. Daytime temperatures could reach 115° F (46° C), but at night they shivered in water-soaked clothing and blankets. Firewood was scarce, so sometimes they could not huddle by the warmth of a fire or cook their food. The men were hungry and tired, and their strength was weakening.

On July 29, Powell and his crew entered a new canyon, which they named Glen Canyon after the stands of oak found along its shoreline. At the canyon's mouth they came across the ruins of an ancient Indian dwelling, which Powell believed once stood three stories high. The ground around it was an archaeologist's delight, strewn with flints, arrowheads, and pottery fragments. It did not take a professional archaeologist to realize that at one time the empty countryside along the Colorado River had been well populated. Later they came across more ruins that included a stairway cut into the rock face of the canyon wall, leading up to what Powell decided must have been an ancient watchtower. Powell speculated that "nomadic tribes were sweeping down" on the people who left these ruins and artifacts, "and they resorted to these cliffs and canyons for safety." These were probably sites associated with Anasazi or Ancestral Puebloan Indians. Twentieth-century archaeologists concluded they had lived in the region from A.D. 700 to about 1150. They had abandoned the settled towns, or pueblos, they built into the canyon for unknown reasons. The Hopi Indians still to be found in the region are believed to be descendants of the Anasazi.

August 3 brought the expedition to another historic site, a place known as the Crossing of the Fathers. This is the ford on the Colorado where Spanish priests Father Silvestre Vélez de Escalante and Father Anastasio Dominguez crossed the river in 1776. On the following day, they reached Marble Canyon, named for the rock formation that stands out along the canyon walls.

DISCONTENT GROWS

On August 10, Powell's expedition reached the mouth of the river the Spanish called the Colorado Chiquito (the Little Colorado). Here they halted again to make scientific measurements, finding further evidence of ancient Native American civilization, including ruins, pottery fragments, and rock drawings known as petroglyphs. There was not enough food or other supplies. Powell was still taking too much time with scientific diversions, as far as the men were concerned, forever stopping to climb the walls of the steep canyons, take barometric readings, and gather rock specimens. "The men are uneasy and discontented and eager to move on," Bradley wrote in his journal on August 11. "If the Major does not do something soon I fear the consequences, but he is contented and seems to think that biscuit made of sour and musty flour and a few dried apples is enough to sustain a laboring man. If he can only study geology he will be happy without food or shelter. . . ." Powell did not realize it, but the next two weeks would bring the greatest challenges.

Powell and his men pushed off onto the river on the morning of August 13. They moved quickly. The canyon sides towered above them. Their rapid progress came to an abrupt halt when they came to a falls, with rapids and boulders strewn in the river below. They had to portage, or carry, their boats around on the narrow shores of the canyon. Then there were more rapids to run. They camped that night in a cave by the water's edge.

August 14 brought more of the same. They could not relax for a moment: "The canyon is narrower than we have ever before seen it; the water is swifter; there are but few broken rocks in the channel; but the walls are set, on either side, with pinnacles and crags; and sharp angular buttresses, bristling with wind and wave-polished spires, extend far out into the river." And then, at about 11 A.M., they came to the greatest obstacle so far. "[W]e hear a great roar ahead, and approach it very cautiously," Powell wrote.

The sound grows louder and louder as we run, and at last we find ourselves above a long, broken fall, with ledges and pinnacles of rock obstructing the river. There is a descent of, perhaps, seventy-five or eighty feet in a third of a mile, and the rushing waters break into great waves on the rocks, and lash themselves into a mad, white foam. We can land just above them, but there is no foothold on either side by which we can make a portage . . . we must run the rapid, or abandon the river. There is no hesitation. We step into our boats, push off and away we go, first on smooth but swift water, then we strike a glassy wave, and ride to its top, down again into the trough, up again on a higher wave, and down and up on waves higher and still higher, until we strike one just as it curls back, and a breaker rolls over our little boat.

The river, they discovered, curved northward time and again. Some days they made good progress. They traveled 20 miles (32 km), for example, on August 21. But there were many difficult portages. They were down to their last bag of flour. On August 26 they stole 10 squashes from a garden. They traveled 35 miles (56 km) that day. Powell expressed the hope that "[a] few days like this and we are out of prison."

On August 27, they reached a new set of rapids. These were the worst yet. George Bradley wrote in his journal: "The billows are huge. . . . The spectacle is appalling to us." There was no way to portage around them. To continue, the men would have to ride through the rapids in their leaky boats. "There is discontent in camp tonight . . . ," Bradley wrote.

A PARTING OF THE WAYS

The Howland brothers and Bill Dunn decided that they had had enough of the dark canyon, of the dangerous river, and of Powell's leadership. They announced that they would prefer to take their chances climbing out of the canyon and striking off overland toward a Mormon settlement called St. George. That was a 70-mile (113-km) hike, a long way to travel across desert. Powell tried to persuade them to abandon the plan. He believed it was only 45 miles (72 km) by river until they would be out of the Grand Canyon. Once they reached the canyon's end, they would be in easy striking distance of white settlements. Still, the Howlands and Bill Dunn wanted no more of Powell's expedition or the Colorado River. Powell was no less determined to continue. "[F]or years I have been contemplating this trip," he wrote. "To leave the exploration unfinished, to say that there is a part of the canyon which I cannot explore, having already almost accomplished it, is more than I am willing to acknowledge."

The Howland brothers and Dunn left on the morning of August 28 and were never seen again. It would be many months before Powell would learn of their unhappy fate. Hiking cross-country, they were reported to have encountered a band of Paiute Indians who, wrongly

The Powell Expedition spent three months exploring the Colorado River area, including Toroweap Point in the Grand Canyon (*above*). Named by Powell in 1869, this 3,000-foot (914-meter) unfenced cliff is the lowest viewpoint in the Grand Canyon.

suspecting them of having raped and murdered a Native American woman, killed all three of them. Another theory blames the murder on local Mormons, who may have considered the three men to be spies.

Powell and his five remaining companions got ready to resume their journey in two boats, abandoning the *Emma Dean* by the riverside. To lighten their load, they also left behind their barometers and the mineral and fossil specimens Powell had collected along the way. Powell took a place on the *Maid of the Canyon* with two others and pushed off:

> We glide rapidly along the foot of the wall, just grazing one great rock, then pull out a little into the chute of the second fall and plunge over it. The open compartment [of the boat] is filled when we strike the first wave below, but we cut through it, and then the men pull with all their power toward the left wall and swing clear of the dangerous rock below all right. We are scarcely a minute in running [the rapids], and find that, although it looked bad from above, we have passed many places that were worse.

The second boat made it through as well. Had the Howlands and Dunn only remained, they would have survived to share in the moment of triumph. On the next day, August 29, the Colorado River Exploring Expedition sailed out of the Grand Canyon and entered the rolling countryside of the region known as the Grand Wash (much of the region is now submerged beneath the waters of Lake Mead). After 99 days on the river, during which they traveled 1,000 miles (1,609 km) of mostly uncharted territory, they were back on the map. They had conquered the Colorado. It was a great individual achievement for Powell, as leader of the expedition. But, as Powell and his men were repeatedly reminded, others had gone before them. They crossed the paths of many earlier explorers, including priests such as Fathers Escalante and Dominguez, mountain men such as William H. Ashley, and military men such as John C. Frémont. The exploration of the "Great Unknown" of western North America was, above all else, a collective effort.

2

Thomas Jefferson's Other Explorers

ON MAY 14, 1804, A PARTY OF EXPLORERS COMMANDED BY U.S. Army captain Meriwether Lewis began a journey up the Missouri River. Lewis's co-commander was William Clark, and their journey became known to history as the Lewis and Clark Expedition. It could have just as easily been called the Jefferson Expedition, because the plan was the idea of President Thomas Jefferson. He had for many years wanted to discover a water route across North America, linking the Atlantic and Pacific oceans. "The object of your mission," Jefferson wrote to Lewis in June 1803, "is to explore the Missouri river, & such principal stream of it, as by it's [sic] course and communication with the waters of the Pacific ocean, whether the Columbia, Oregan, Colorado or any other river may offer the most direct & practicable water communication across this continent for the purposes of commerce."

Lewis and Clark would fail in the mission assigned them by Jefferson to find a "practicable" water route across the continent. They failed because no such route existed. The headwaters of the Missouri, high in the Rocky Mountains, did not lie anywhere near those of the Columbia or any other river that emptied into the Pacific. There was no "height of land" that served as the source for all the West's major rivers. As for the Rockies, they were not a simple chain of ridges like the Appalachian and Blue Ridge mountains of the East but a region of mountains that rose in places to more than twice the height of the highest Appalachians. Once across the Rockies, travelers heading west still faced many hundreds of miles of difficult travel, down rapid-flowing rivers, or across barren deserts, and over still more mountains before coming at last to the Pacific Ocean.

Jefferson's mistaken notions about western geography nonetheless proved very fruitful for the United States. Had he realized the true difficulties of western exploration and travel, he might never have sent Lewis and Clark or any other explorers westward. Though they failed to find the Northwest Passage leading to the riches of Asia, Lewis and Clark achieved much of great importance to the future of their country. They mapped the Missouri, the Columbia, and the Yellowstone rivers. They found passages through the Rocky Mountains. They established contact with Native American tribes like the Shoshone and Nez Perce who had never before seen white people. And they laid the basis for future U.S. territorial claims in the Pacific Northwest. As a result of their epic journey of 1804–1806, they secured for themselves a place in U.S. history as the greatest of North American explorers.

Lewis and Clark's fame, although much deserved, has obscured the efforts of the other explorers who headed west in the years of Thomas Jefferson's presidency. President Jefferson was personally fond of Meriwether Lewis and held out great hopes for the success of his expedition. Nonetheless, he intended the Lewis and Clark Expedition to be just a part of a coordinated effort to learn more about the vast, unexplored regions west of the Mississippi. Meriwether Lewis, William Clark, Doctor John Sibley, William Dunbar, and others were all part of Jefferson's ambitious program of exploration, engaged in what might collectively be labeled the Jefferson Expeditions. With the possible exception of John F. Kennedy and the space race of the 1960s, no president of the United States has ever been as committed to using the power of the federal government for the purpose of exploration as Thomas Jefferson.

THE LOUISIANA PURCHASE

Jefferson was convinced that the successful growth of this new democratic government that had been launched in 1776 depended upon westward expansion. The American West, he hoped, would prove a land of fertile soil and abundant rainfall, just waiting to be settled and developed by farmers. Although he was a wealthy man, a plantation owner, and slave owner, Thomas Jefferson saw himself as a champion of the common people. In the United States, unlike Europe, land

Thomas Jefferson supported exploration of western North America as the third president of the United States. His goal was to explore uncharted regions of the Louisiana Territory, which the United States bought from France in 1803.

was abundant and available to all who would till it, however humble their origins. In the United States, unlike Europe, no one need live in crowded, disease-ridden cities if they preferred a healthy, virtuous life close to the soil. Independent, property-owning farmers, Jefferson believed, were the ideal citizens of a free and self-governing country like the United States.

In 1803, Jefferson asked James Monroe to go to Paris to take part in the negotiations that led a few months later to the purchase of the Louisiana Territory from the French government. Jefferson made clear to Monroe what he thought the stakes were: "On the event of this mission depends the future destinies of this republic." On July 3, 1803, President Jefferson received official confirmation that the government of France was prepared to sell the Louisiana Territory to the United States. For the bargain price of $15 million, American negotiators in Paris added 828,000 square miles (1,332,536 sq km) to the territory of the United States, doubling its size.

Although the Louisiana Territory was thought to include all the lands west of the Mississippi that drained into that great river basin, no one at the time was quite sure what that meant. When Robert Livingston, one of the American negotiators in Paris, asked the French foreign minister Charles-Maurice de Talleyrand-Périgord to describe the extent of the lands being conveyed by sale to the United States, Talleyrand replied, "I can give you no direction. You have made a noble bargain for yourselves and I suppose you will make the most of it."

Jefferson decided that Lewis and Clark would explore the lands along the Missouri River, which would take them to the northern edge of the Louisiana Territory. But Jefferson also wanted to know about the Louisiana Territory's southern boundaries. Even before the Louisiana Purchase, Americans had begun to show interest in the Spanish province of Texas. In 1791 Philip Nolan, an Irish immigrant to the United States and a friend of Jefferson, had received permission from Spanish authorities to make a trip to Texas. He went to buy horses from the Comanche Indians to bring back and sell in Louisiana. He spent several years in the province, traveling as far south as San Antonio in 1794. But Nolan seemed to have more than horse-trading in mind. Spanish authorities grew suspicious of his exploring and mapmaking, as well as his association with prominent Americans. In 1800, Nolan led a small expedition of well-armed Americans to found a fort in Texas along the Brazos River. Spanish authorities dispatched troops from Nacogdoches to arrest him. In a fight on March 21, 1801, Nolan was killed. His followers were marched south and sentenced to hard labor in a Spanish prison. Nolan was the first of what would be called the "filibusters," Americans acting on their own (or with hidden support from the U.S. government) to undermine Spanish rule in Texas.

Jefferson took the oath of office just two weeks before Nolan's death at Spanish hands. It would be some months before he learned of Nolan's fate. He did not want conflict with the Spanish, but he did want to know more about Texas and the lands beyond. So he turned to other explorers for help, starting with William Dunbar.

THE DUNBAR-HUNTER EXPEDITION

William Dunbar was born around 1750 in Morayshire, Scotland, to wealthy parents. He was well educated, graduating from King's College in Aberdeen, Scotland, in 1767. He was trained as a chemist and botanist, and immigrated to Britain's North American colonies in 1771. Settling first in Philadelphia, Dunbar then moved to West Florida and finally to the Mississippi River, establishing a plantation in 1792 near present-day Natchez, Mississippi.

Dunbar was an inventor as well as a planter. He set up a business to manufacture barrel staves (wood strips that form the side of a barrel) and developed the use of square-shaped cotton bales that became the standard method of packing the South's principal export crop for transportation. He also pioneered the study of meteorology in the Mississippi Valley. He was a man of thought and action, a combination that greatly appealed to Thomas Jefferson.

When he lived in West Florida, Dunbar had served as surveyor general and had become acquainted with surveyor and astronomer Andrew Ellicott (who taught Meriwether Lewis the art of celestial navigation at Jefferson's request). Ellicott introduced Dunbar to Jefferson. The latter two men maintained a friendly correspondence over the years, including such topics as Native American sign language and fossil remains found west of the Mississippi.

In March 1804, Jefferson wrote to Dunbar to ask him to lead an expedition to explore the southern tributaries of the Mississippi, aiding in the preparation of "a map of Louisiana which in its contours and main waters will be perfectly accurate." Jefferson was particularly interested in the course of the Red River, which emptied its waters into the Mississippi after flowing east through Texas. Jefferson hoped that the Red might prove the southern counterpart of the Missouri River to the north and flow all the way from the Rockies. Jefferson also wanted Dunbar to act as a diplomat, announcing to the Native American tribes along the Red and Arkansas rivers that, thanks to the Louisiana Purchase, they had a new "great white father" who lived in a place called Washington, D.C.

Dunbar agreed, but Jefferson began having second thoughts. He had heard from Osage Indians visiting Washington that the projected mission up the Red River might inflame both Native American and Spanish resentment. Jefferson decided to postpone the exploration of the Red for the moment. Instead he asked Dunbar to lead a party up the Ouachita River, a tributary of the Red River, as a kind of test run for a more ambitious journey later. George Hunter, a Philadelphia chemist, joined Dunbar's expedition at Jefferson's request.

On October 14, 1804, the party, known as the Dunbar-Hunter Expedition, set off from St. Catherine's Landing, south of Natchez. In addition to its two civilian leaders, the expedition included a U.S. Army sergeant and 12 soldiers, plus Hunter's son George, a slave belonging to Dunbar, and a guide. They made their way up the Mississippi to the mouth of the Red River, then upstream to the Black River. From there they went to the mouth of the Ouachita River, following the Ouachita as far as it could be navigated. They took careful astronomical readings to map their way, as the river wound its way through northern Louisiana and on into Arkansas.

The high point of the expedition came when they reached a region of thermal hot springs (present-day Hot Springs, Arkansas) in early December. Though the springs had long been known to the Native Americans, and known to Europeans since their discovery by Spanish explorer Hernando de Soto in 1541, the men in the Dunbar-Hunter party were the first Americans to enjoy the pleasure of bathing in them. Dunbar and his men were in no hurry to leave. The explorers spent a month at the hot springs before setting out on their return journey in early January.

Dunbar wrote to Jefferson soon after his return to Natchez, sending along his observations about the hot springs. In spring 1805, Jefferson had yet to receive any reports from the Lewis and Clark Expedition. Therefore, he was quite pleased that the other party he

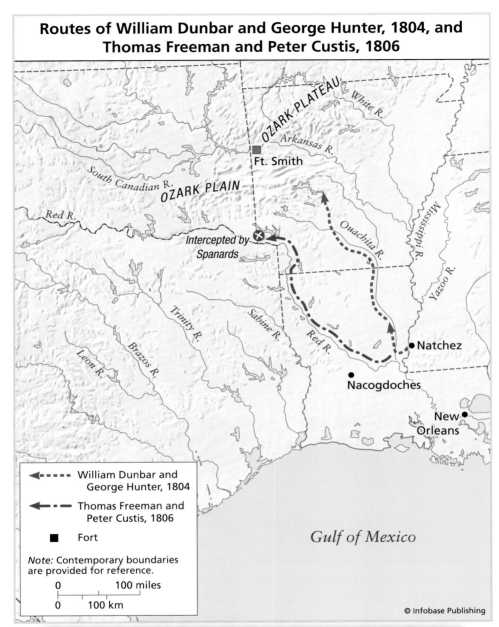

Routes of William Dunbar and George Hunter, 1804, and Thomas Freeman and Peter Custis, 1806

White R.

OZARK PLATEAU

Arkansas R.

■ Ft. Smith

South Canadian R.

OZARK PLAIN

Red R.

Intercepted by Spanards

Ouachita R.

Mississippi R.

Yazoo R.

Trinity R.

Sabine R.

Red R.

Leon R.

Brazos R.

● Natchez

● Nacogdoches

New ● Orleans

◄----- William Dunbar and
George Hunter, 1804

◄--- Thomas Freeman and
Peter Custis, 1806

■ Fort

Note: Contemporary boundaries
are provided for reference.

0   100 miles
0   100 km

Gulf of Mexico

© Infobase Publishing

Jefferson authorized four expeditions to explore the territory gained with
the Louisiana Purchase, including the Dunbar-Hunter Expedition of 1804
and the Freeman-Custis Expedition of 1806.

had sent out to explore the new Louisiana Territory had enjoyed at least a limited success in exploring one of the minor southern tributaries of the Mississippi. "Those who come after us will extend the ramifications as they become acquainted with them," Jefferson wrote in a letter to Dunbar on May 25, 1805, praising his expedition, "and fill up the canvas we begin."

THE FREEMAN-CUSTIS EXPEDITION

It was not long before another party set out to help "fill up the canvas" of the Mississippi's southern tributaries. A year after the Dunbar-Hunter Expedition's return, Jefferson decided it was time to return to his initial plan of mapping the Red River to its source. Dunbar was uninterested, so this expedition would be led by Colonel Thomas Freeman, a civil engineer and surveyor. Freeman was accompanied by Peter Custis, a medical student at the University of Pennsylvania. The Freeman-Custis Expedition included army officers Captain Richard Spark and Lieutenant Enoch Humphreys and a group of soldiers—40 men in all. On April 19, 1806, they set off up the Mississippi River from Fort Adams, south of Natchez. They reached the American outpost of Campti on the Red River by June 7. There they received a warning sent by courier from federal agent John Sibley, a physician living in Natchitoches, Louisiana. Sibley, another of Jefferson's scientific correspondents, had learned that the Spanish authorities in the Southwest were on the lookout for Freeman's party and had sent patrols to intercept them. Although concerned about the possibility of a clash with the Spanish, Sibley himself followed his courier upriver to join the party.

Freeman and his men had orders to turn back only if they met a superior Spanish force, so they pressed on up the Red River. They encouraged the Native Americans they met along the river to take down the Spanish flags they displayed in their villages and gave them U.S. flags to fly in their place. The Spanish did not accept this challenge to their authority. On July 29, Spanish troops intercepted the Freeman party at a spot on the Red River known ever since as Spanish Bluff, about 30 miles (48 km) northwest of present-day Texarkana, Texas. The Spanish commander bluntly told the Americans that they were trespassing and had better head back to their own territory at once. Freeman's party was badly outnumbered, so the expedition turned around and headed home. Jefferson's hopes for exploring and

THE OPENING OF THE AMERICAN SOUTHWEST

At the start of the nineteenth century, explorers from the United States were just beginning to find their way into the American Southwest. But this was a region known to other European explorers long before the Americans showed up. In 1540, not quite 50 years after Christopher Columbus's first voyage, the Spanish explorer Francisco Vásquez de Coronado had led an expedition of 1,000 men north from Mexico into what were later to be the states of Arizona and New Mexico. He ultimately pushed on as far as Kansas before returning to Mexico in 1542. As early as 1598, 200 Spanish families followed the Basque nobleman Juan de Oñate northward from Mexico to form San Juan de los Caballeros, the first Spanish settlement in northern New Mexico. In contrast, it would be nearly a decade before the first permanent British settlement, Jamestown, Virginia, was established on the Atlantic coast of North America. It would take the descendents of those British settlements another two centuries before they began to approach the borders of the territory the Spanish had first explored and settled in the sixteenth century.

The Americans would make up for lost time in the nineteenth century, and the Spanish were well aware of the threat. Fifteen years before the Louisiana Purchase, Spain's viceroy in Mexico, Manuel Antonio Florez, offered a grim prophecy for the future of the Spanish empire in North America. "We ought not to be surprized," he warned the Spanish government in 1788, "that the English colonies of America, now being an independent Republic, should carry out the design of finding a safe port on the Pacific and of attempting to sustain it by crossing the immense country of the continent above our possessions of Texas, New Mexico, and California."

mapping the southern border of the Louisiana Territory would not be realized for the time being.

ZEBULON MONTGOMERY PIKE

After Lewis and Clark, the best-known explorer of the Jeffersonian era was undoubtedly Zebulon Montgomery Pike. Pike was born in Lamberton, New Jersey, in 1779, the son of an American military officer. Following his father's example, Pike joined the U.S. Army at age 15 and served on the Ohio frontier in the 1790s. A skilled outdoorsman and hunter, he taught himself French and Spanish, as well as a smattering of mathematics and science.

It often took a powerful supporter to help a young officer rise to prominence in the small U.S. peacetime army of the early nineteenth century. Zebulon Montgomery Pike, for better and worse, found his own patron in General James Wilkinson. A Revolutionary War veteran who had fought at Bunker Hill, Wilkinson was appointed commander of the U.S. Army in 1797. In 1805, Jefferson appointed him governor of the upper Louisiana Territory. But Jefferson did not know that for many years Wilkinson had been secretly employed as an agent of the Spanish government, and Wilkinson had warned the Spanish authorities in New Orleans of the impending Lewis and Clark Expedition. To complicate matters further, Wilkinson may have been plotting to betray his Spanish paymasters as well as his own country. In 1805, he and former vice president Aaron Burr hatched a complicated plot to split off the trans-Appalachian states and territories from the United States and perhaps link them up with an independent Mexico as a separate country. Had they succeeded, the subsequent history of the United States, and indeed of the world, might have been very different.

PIKE'S FIRST EXPEDITION

In summer 1805, Wilkinson ordered Pike, then stationed at Fort Kaskaskia in the Illinois Territory, to lead a scientific and diplomatic expedition up the Mississippi River. Pike was to map the upper stretches of the great river, contact and gather information on the tribes who lived along its waters, and find the river's headwaters before winter.

Pike kept a daily expedition journal. "Sailed from my encampment near Saint Louis," Pike wrote after the first day's voyage of the Upper Mississippi Exploring Expedition:

> [A]t 4 Oclock P.M. on Friday the 9th Augt. 1805, with one Sergt. [sergeant] Two corporals and 17 privates in a Keel Boat 70 feet long; provisiond for four months; with orders to explore the source of the Mississippi making a general survey of the river and its boundaries, and its productions, both in the Animal, vegitable and mineral creation; also to include observations on the savage inhabitants of its Banks—Water very rapid—encamped on the E. side at the head of and Island[.]

At first they made rapid progress upriver, blessed with favorable winds. By September 4, the expedition reached the settlement of Prairie du Chien, a trading center near the mouth of the Wisconsin River. Although in 1805 Prairie du Chien lay in what had become U.S. territory, most of the inhabitants of the settlement still looked to British Canada as their protector. Pike noted the results: "[I]t is astonishing to me, what a dread the Indians have of the Americans in this quarter. I have frequently seen them go round Islands to avoid meeting my Boat. It appears evident to me that the Traders have taken great pains to impress on the minds of the Savages, an idea of our being a very vindictive, ferocious and War like people. This impression was given no doubt with an evil intention . . ."

The Mississippi had become too shallow and rock-filled to take it any further upriver, so the expedition abandoned the keelboat at Prairie du Chien. From there they proceeded in canoes purchased or hired from the local inhabitants. By September 21, Pike noted in his journal that the river "became so very narrow . . . that I once crossed [it] in Forty Strokes of my oars . . ."

Pike passed out gifts and smoked peace pipes with the Native American tribes he encountered along the river. On September 23, at a site near present-day Minneapolis, Pike held a council with chiefs from the Dakota Sioux tribe. On behalf of the U.S. government, he purchased from them more than 150,000 acres (60,702 hectares) of land on either side of the river. In exchange, the tribe received $200 worth of presents

During an expedition to locate the headwaters of the Mississippi River, Zebulon Pike purchased more than 150,000 acres of land from the chiefs of the Dakota Sioux tribe. In this early twentieth century photograph by Edward S. Curtis, three Dakota Sioux on horseback gaze across the Great Plains.

and 60 gallons of whiskey. Pike's purchase of this land was the first treaty signed by a representative of the U.S. government with tribes living west of the Mississippi.

Despite the onset of cold weather, sickness among his party, leaky boats, dwindling supplies, and his orders from Wilkinson to return to St. Louis before winter, Pike kept heading northward up the river. He had hopes of winning fame as an explorer and too little to show on his first expedition. His actions over the next few months proved that he had more luck than skill as a commander of men in the wilderness.

On October 16, Pike called a temporary halt at the mouth of the Swan River, near present-day Little Falls, Minnesota. Then, after nearly two months' delay, he pushed north again with a party of 12 soldiers, leaving the rest of his men behind in a small stockade they had constructed on the riverbank. Pike and his exploring party took one small canoe with them and dragged wooden sleds along the riverbanks to carry their supplies. Progress was slow and difficult. "Never did I undergo more fatigue," Pike complained on December 23, two weeks after resuming his journey. As for his men, he described them as "poor fellows, who were killing themselves to obey my orders." They observed Christmas Day on the trail, with Pike passing out rations to his men. By this point he was barely able to walk.

They might well have died in the frozen wilderness, leaving no trace of their existence. Fortunately, on January 2, 1806, Pike and his men encountered two traders from the North West Company, one of the two major Canadian fur companies. They led the Americans to the North West Company trading post at Cedar Lake, near present-day Aitken, Minnesota. From this point on, Pike was not so much exploring new territory as enjoying the hospitality of the well-established British traders. North West trader James Grant invited Pike to accompany him farther upcountry. They reached their next stop, the Lake De Sable trading post, on January 13, and was given a warm welcome.

Refreshed, they set out again upriver. On January 31, Pike came to a fork in the river. He decided that its western branch must lead to the headwaters of the Mississippi River. On the afternoon of February 1, 1805, they reached Leech Lake. "I will not attempt to describe my feeling on the accomplishment of my voyage," Pike wrote in his journal, "this being the main source of the Mississippi." But he was mistaken. The eastern fork, leading to Lake Itasca, led to the actual headwaters of the Mississippi. At Leech Lake, Pike and his men once more enjoyed the hospitality of North West Company traders, who maintained an outpost on the shores of the lake. But Pike was not so gracious a guest this time. He had his soldiers shoot down the Union Jack that flew over the trading post.

On February 18, Pike and his men headed south. When they rejoined the rest of their party at the stockade on the Swan River, they found things in a bad way. Sergeant Henry Kennerman, whom Pike had left in command, had traded off many of their supplies to the local Native Americans. Furious, Pike demoted him to private and denounced his treachery in the journal: "[T]hat man [Kennerman] was squandering the Flour, Pork and Liquor away during the winter. Whilst we were starving with hunger and cold."

Spring was slow in coming to the upper Mississippi. On April 7, the river was finally clear of ice, and Pike and his men resumed their journey southward. They reached St. Louis on April 30, having covered 5,000 miles (8,046 km) in under nine months. The British flag, Pike happily reported to Wilkinson, "has given place to that of the United States wherever we past . . ."

President Jefferson had been informed by General Wilkinson of Pike's mission only after his departure up the Mississippi. Still the president approved of Wilkinson's plan. In his report to Congress in December 1806, Jefferson declared, "Very useful additions have . . . been made to our knowledge of the Mississippi by Lieutenant Pike, who has ascended to its source. . . ." That was a generous assessment, for Pike had failed to discover any significant geographical features previously unknown to mapmakers. He also failed to secure the allegiance of the Native American tribes of the upper Mississippi (most of whom sided with the British a few years later in the War of 1812).

PIKE'S SECOND EXPEDITION

Pike was given a new assignment a mere two months after his return to St. Louis. Wilkinson ordered him to take an expedition westward to the Rocky Mountains to find the headwaters of the Red River. The Freeman-Custis party had not yet returned from its own attempt to reach those headwaters, but Pike would follow a different route on his mission. He was ordered to head out overland across the central plains to the southern Rockies, then make his way back eastward along the Red River.

Once again Wilkinson was acting on his own. He did not inform President Jefferson of the expedition until after Pike's departure. Wilkinson's orders to Pike specified that he should "move with great circumspection" as he neared Spanish territory in the Southwest, in order to avoid a border incident since "it is the desire of the President, to cultivate the Friendship & Harmonious Intercourse, of all the Nations of the Earth, & particularly our near neighbours the Spaniards." Provoking a border incident, however, may have been exactly what Wilkinson had in mind. Wilkinson and his co-conspirator Aaron Burr hoped for an American war with Spain for control of the Southwest. This would give them the opportunity to carry out their plan to set up an independent western country under their own control. Pike was to be an unwitting pawn in Wilkinson and Burr's designs.

Pike's expedition set off up the Missouri River in two keelboats on July 15, 1806. This time he had 22 men under his command, including 17 enlisted men who had accompanied him up the Mississippi the previous year and two new volunteers. He even brought along the disgraced Private (formerly Sergeant) Henry Kennerman. His expedition also included another officer, Lieutenant James Biddle Wilkinson (General Wilkinson's son), an interpreter, and Dr. John H. Robinson, a physician who may have been working as an agent for Wilkinson.

On the first stage of the journey, Pike's party escorted 51 Osage Indians back to their homes in Kansas. The Osage had been captured by Potawatomi Indians and then released into the custody of the U.S. government in St. Louis. They were being returned to their village as a goodwill gesture by the U.S. authorities. The Pike party headed up the Missouri to the mouth of the Osage River, and then followed the Osage to Grand Osage Village, near present-day Osceola, Missouri. They reached the village on August 15.

After holding a council with the Osage chiefs, Pike and his men headed west on horseback, leaving their keelboats behind. Before long, their party was reduced in size by one man: The unreliable Private Kennerman deserted. On September 25, they reached a Pawnee village on the Republic River, near present-day Red Cloud, Nebraska. The Pawnee chief White Wolf warned Pike that the Spanish had been alerted to his expedition and were out looking for him with a large body of mounted troops. The Pawnee seemed to be sympathetic to the Spanish. He insisted they take down the Spanish flags in their village and replace them with the Stars and Stripes. Then he delivered a defiant speech designed to impress his Pawnee listeners: "The young warriors of his *great American father were not women* to be turned back by *words. . . .*"

While staying with the Pawnee, Pike learned from a visiting French trader of Lewis and Clark's recent return to St. Louis from their expedition to the Pacific. As Pike recalled, "this diffused general joy through our party." It may also have intensified Pike's personal ambition to achieve similar glory. On October 7, Pike and his men set off, heading south toward the Arkansas River. At the Great Bend of the Arkansas River, the party divided. Lieutenant Wilkinson set off with four soldiers down the Arkansas River in bullboats (wood-framed vessels covered in animal skins), carrying dispatches and maps back to St. Louis. Meanwhile, the rest of the party under Pike continued westward on horseback.

As they headed west, Pike and his men feasted on the plentiful buffalo of the Kansas plains. Their horses were not as lucky. Once again, as in the previous year on the Mississippi, Pike pressed on when a more cautious commander would have settled in for winter.

PIKE'S PEAK

On November 11, still following the Arkansas River, Pike's party crossed the present-day border of Kansas and Colorado. On November 15, Pike wrote, "At about two o'clock in the afternoon I thought I could distinguish a mountain to our right, which appeared like a small blue cloud. . . . When our small party arrived on the hill they with one accord gave three *cheers* to the *Mexican mountains*." What he called the Mexican mountains was the Front Range of the Rockies, still 150 miles (241 km) distant. The stretch of the Rockies passing through Colorado includes 51 mountain summits more than 14,000 feet (4,267 m) high.

On November 23, after a hostile encounter with a party of Pawnee who tried to rob the expedition of horses and guns, Pike halted the journey and built a stockade in what is now Pueblo, Colorado. The following day Pike set off with Dr. Robinson and Privates Brown and Miller to attempt to climb a "Grand Peak" in the mountain range that lay before them. Pike thought he was close enough to climb the mountain and return to camp in a single day. Instead, three days later, they were still approaching the mountain's base. From a hilltop to its southeast (possibly Blue or Black Mountain) Pike gazed up at the snowy summit that was their goal and concluded the mountain was unclimbable. Pike's "Grand Peak" would later be known as "Pike's Peak." At 14,110 feet (4,300 m), it is not the highest of Colorado's mountains, but because it stands apart from surrounding peaks, it is highly visible from the Great Plains.

Returning to the stockade on the Arkansas River, Pike gathered up the rest of his party and pressed on. On December 5, they reached a river junction in present-day Canon City, Colorado, where the Arkansas was joined by several smaller creeks. When the creek became a mere brook, Pike mistakenly decided he had found the headwaters of the Arkansas. He spent the next several weeks in a useless search for the headwaters of the Red River. His wanderings through the mountainous terrain were so erratic and so poorly described in his journal that historians who later tried to retrace his steps could never be sure of where Pike and his party had actually gone. On January 5, 1807, to what he described as his "great mortification," Pike found himself back at the same place on the Arkansas River, near present-day Canon City, from which he had led his men a month earlier. It was his twenty-eighth birthday, and, as he confessed in his journal, "most fervently did I hope never to pass another so miserably."

Pike's men were in a bad way. Their commander made matters worse by dividing his small party. He decided to build another fortification, leaving behind the horses, some of the baggage, and two of his men. On January 14, with 19 men, Pike headed south into the Sangre de Cristo Mountains, still in search of the elusive headwaters of the Red River. They made it over the mountains but suffered terribly in the effort. By January 19, Pike reported, "I had become extremely weak and faint, being the fourth day, since we had received sustenance; all of which we were marching hard and the last night had scarcely closed our eyes to sleep." He left more men behind, to catch up later on their own (miraculously, despite the bitter cold, short rations, and frostbitten feet, none of those left behind would die). He threatened another soldier, who had complained that he had not eaten in three days, with "*instant* death" by firing squad. On February 1, he had his men build yet another fortification near present-day Alamosa, Colorado, on a branch of the Rio Grande. He mistakenly believed this to be the long-sought Red River.

At this point the mysterious Dr. Robinson headed off on his own to ride to the Spanish city of Santa Fe, where he said he had private business to carry out. Whatever his business may have been, Robinson's arrival in Santa Fe seems to have tipped off the Spanish authorities to the presence of U.S. intruders in their neighborhood. On February 26, 100 mounted Spanish soldiers showed up at Pike's small fort and took him and his men into custody. The men Pike had left behind in the mountains were soon rounded up as well. Pike and the main party reached Santa Fe under guard on the evening of March 3. There he was interrogated by the governor of New Mexico, Joaquin del Real Alencaster. Pike maintained that he had strayed into Spanish territory by mistake, but he was unable to convince the governor of his innocence.

From Santa Fe, Pike and his men were taken south to Chihuahua, Mexico. The Spanish were entirely within their rights to arrest Pike and his men, but they were not prepared to go to war with the United States over this intrusion into their territory. If Wilkinson's purpose in

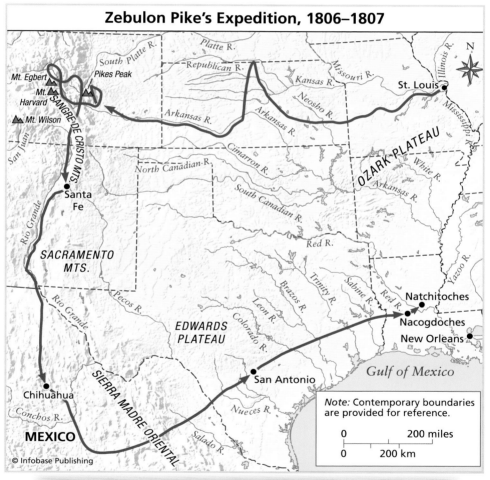

Zebulon Pike's Expedition, 1806–1807

During his second expedition, Zebulon Pike was arrested and taken into custody by Spanish authorities. He and his men were taken under guard from Santa Fe to Chihuahua. During the trip, Pike kept his eyes and ears open and was able to relay information about the New Mexico Territory to the U.S. government.

sending Pike on his mission had been to launch such a conflict, he had not succeeded. On June 30, 1807, Pike, Dr. Robinson, and six enlisted men were escorted across Texas and released into the custody of American authorities at Fort Claiborne in Natchitoches, Louisiana. Other members of the party were later released. "Language cannot express the gaiety of my heart when I once beheld the standards of my country waved aloft," Pike said of his return.

PIKE'S ACHIEVEMENTS

Pike expected to receive a hero's welcome from a grateful country. In a book he published in 1810 describing his two expeditions, he compared his achievements as an explorer with those of Lewis and Clark. But his countrymen did not agree. By the time Pike had returned to the United States, Aaron Burr had been arrested on charges of treason. Burr was acquitted in 1807, but he left the country in disgrace. General Wilkinson fell under well-deserved suspicion, and Pike's association with Wilkinson did him little good in public opinion.

Considered on its own merits, Pike's expedition paled in comparison with Lewis and Clark's. Although it filled in some blank spaces on the map, the most lasting effect of the expedition was its contribution to yet another geographical misconception about the nature of the American West. "This vast plains of the western hemisphere," Pike wrote in his 1810 book, "may become in time as celebrated as the sandy deserts of Africa; for I saw in my route, in various places, tracts of many leagues where the wind had thrown up the sand in all the fanciful forms of the ocean's rolling wave, and on which not a speck of vegetable matter existed." Thus was born the myth of the Great American Desert.

Pike was more successful as a spy than as a scientific explorer. He kept his eyes and ears open while in captivity and gathered detailed information on Spanish troop deployments in New Spain. (New Spain was the Spanish territories that included present-day California, southwestern United States, Mexico, Central America except Panama, the Caribbean, and the Philippines.) As it turned out, however, the United States would not go to war in the Southwest until 1846, when it fought an independent Mexico. Pike's espionage was of no use by then.

Pike remained in the army, and in the War of 1812 he was given command of the 15th U.S. Infantry. He died in battle on April 27, 1813, commanding U.S. forces in the Battle of York. After his heroic death, he rose in public opinion. The first steamboat to travel up the Mississippi River and arrive in St. Louis in 1817 was named the *Pike*. Pike's Peak in the Rocky Mountain Front Range would later become a favorite American tourist destination, with a cog railway and a road built to its top. It was after a visit to the summit in 1893 that Katherine Lee Bates wrote the words to "America the Beautiful." Pike's discovery was the original inspiration for the famous lyric about "purple mountains' majesty."

By the time Thomas Jefferson stepped down from the presidency in 1809, the United States was double the size it had been when he had taken office in 1801. Some of the new Louisiana Territory had been explored, but much remained unknown. The next great phase of western exploration was undertaken by individuals and companies out for private gain in the era of the mountain men.

3

Fur Traders and the Exploration of the Western Frontier

HAD THERE BEEN NO BEAVERS IN NORTH AMERICA, THE FULL exploration of the American West might have been delayed by years. In the early decades of the nineteenth century, a few hardy explorers, most of them military men, traveled in the western territories of the United States on officially supported expeditions. Thousands more, though, headed there on their own initiative, caring little about exploration for its own sake. They did care a great deal about the price a beaver pelt would fetch in New York, Montreal, or London.

The fur trade was a vast international enterprise linking North America with Europe and Asia. The men who gathered the furs in the western American wilderness did not, for the most part, keep systematic records of their exploration. Through word of mouth and accounts in the popular press, the discoveries of these "mountain men" contributed to increasing the geographical knowledge of the American West. The paths the mountain men followed along riverbanks and across open plains and the passes they crossed in the Rocky Mountains would soon be followed by tens of thousands of pioneers and settlers along the Oregon and Santa Fe trails.

ORIGINS OF THE FUR TRADE

For 1,000 years before the Louisiana Purchase, elaborate trade networks linked distant Native American tribes. Shells, dried fish, and whale oil harvested by tribes living along the Pacific Northwest were traded for furs, turquoise, and obsidian cutting tools by tribes living east of the

Rocky Mountains. Meanwhile, the Native Peoples of the Plains traded buffalo robes for corn grown by tribes living along the Missouri River. The arrival of the Spanish in the Southwest, the French in Canada, and the English along the Atlantic seacoast and the shores of Hudson Bay built upon these existing trade networks. The Europeans added tools and weapons fashioned of iron, brightly colored beads, tobacco, brandy, and blanket cloth to the list of goods exchanged.

The most valuable resources the Native Americans had to offer the white traders were furs, including the pelts of bears, foxes, martens, wildcats, wolverines, muskrats, minks, and otters. But of all the furs of North American mammals, the one valued most was the beaver. The fine short underlayer of beaver fur, its "wool," could be used to make felt, a cloth produced by the pressing or treating of animal hair with chemicals. The felt made from beaver wool was not only waterproof and durable but soft to the touch, ideal for making hats. From the start of the seventeenth century until well into the nineteenth century, such hats were all the rage among the fashionable gentlemen of London and Paris.

French settlers in Canada were in the lead of this profit-inspired exploration of the North American interior. Jacques Cartier made three expeditions up the St. Lawrence River between 1534 and 1541. Like many others who came to North America in those years, he came looking for gold and the Northwest Passage, and he found neither. What he did find were Native Americans so eager to trade furs for European goods that they literally stripped the fur clothing from their backs. "They bartered all they had to such an extent that all went back naked without anything on them," Cartier wrote of his encounters along the shores of the St. Lawrence on his first trip up the river in 1534, "and they made signs to us that they would return on the morrow with more furs." By 1608, French explorer Samuel de Champlain had established a trading post at what would become the city of Quebec. In decades to come, French *voyageurs* (boatmen) and *coureurs du bois* (literally "runners of the woods," or woodsmen) began making their way westward, in birch-bark canoes, exploring the tributary rivers of the St. Lawrence northward toward Hudson Bay. They reached and crossed the water chain of the Great Lakes, and then looked ever farther to the west for new sources of furs.

From the seventeenth to the nineteenth century, hats made from beaver fur were popular among the most fashionable men of Europe. Pictured is a beaver felt top hat displayed on fur pelts at the Fort Langley National Historic Site in British Columbia, Canada.

The English were relative latecomers to the North American fur trade. With the formation in 1670 of the Company of Adventurers in England Trading into Hudson's Bay (better known as the Hudson's Bay Company), they emerged as fierce rivals to the French merchants of Quebec and Montreal. To the south, the French monopoly on the fur trade west of the Appalachian Mountains was challenged in the 1750s by the appearance of British-American traders in the Ohio Valley; it was one of the causes of the French and Indian War of 1754–1763.

In 1763, with the English victory, Canada was added to the British Empire. The Hudson's Bay Company might have been expected to extend its monopoly over the entire country's trade. Instead, the Hudson's Bay traders found themselves challenged by independent traders and trappers, both English and French. In 1784 a group of merchant traders, some of them French and some Scottish, united to form the North West Company. Their employees would go on to play a significant role in the exploration of western Canada and the Pacific Northwest. Meanwhile in Alaska and farther south along the Pacific coast, the Russians were developing their own fur-trading empire, forming the Russian American Company.

The fur trade in the United States was never as highly organized or centralized as the French and British fur-trading enterprises, despite efforts by the U.S. government to imitate the success of the Hudson's Bay Company. In 1796, Congress passed legislation establishing a system of government-run "factories"—really trading posts on the frontier. But a variety of problems weakened the factories in the face of private competition. The program was abandoned in 1822.

THE CHOUTEAU FAMILY AND THE ST. LOUIS FUR TRADE

Like Quebec and Montreal to the north, the city of St. Louis was founded on the fur trade. In 1763, a New Orleans merchant named Pierre Laclede journeyed up the Mississippi to found a trading post at the river's junction with the Missouri. Accompanying Laclede were a party of workmen and his 14-year-old stepson, Auguste Chouteau. Laclede died in 1778, but his children Auguste and Pierre (Auguste's half-brother) went on to found a family fur-trading dynasty. The "brown gold" of beaver pelts that flowed into the city from the Great Plains and the Rocky Mountains remained the city's most important source of wealth well into the nineteenth century.

When St. Louis passed from Spanish to American control in 1804, the ranks of would-be fur traders from the East increased dramatically. The Chouteaus had no intention of being pushed aside by the English-speaking newcomers and were eager to establish their loyalty and usefulness to the U.S. government. They provided information to Lewis and Clark about what to expect from the Native Americans they would encounter along the Missouri River. Pierre Chouteau's son, Auguste-Pierre, or A.P. Chouteau, as he would be known, was one of the first cadets to be accepted into the newly created U.S. Military Academy at West Point, New York. On his return to St. Louis, A.P. Chouteau served as an aide to the territorial governor, General James Wilkinson. He also made several journeys up the Missouri to trade with the Mandan and Arikara Indians in 1807 and 1808. In 1809, along with his father,

A.P. became a partner in the St. Louis Missouri Fur Company. The various Chouteau enterprises over the next half-century or so would leave the West sprinkled with family place names, from Fort Pierre in South Dakota to Chouteau County in Montana, as well as the town of Choteau, seat of Montana's Teton County.

MANUEL LISA

Apart from the Chouteaus, the most notable figure in the early nineteenth century St. Louis fur trade was Manuel Lisa. Born to Spanish parents in New Orleans in 1772, Lisa moved to St. Louis in 1799. He became the Chouteaus' chief rival in the fur trade. He, too, conferred with Lewis and Clark, though for unknown reasons he aroused Lewis's anger. Captain Lewis denounced Lisa as a "great scoundrel" shortly before setting out up the Missouri in 1804. But Lewis's antagonism to Lisa did not survive the trip, and they established a working relationship on the return of the Corps of Discovery from the Pacific.

Lisa paid careful attention to Lewis and Clark's account of their journey and was quick to follow their path westward. He traveled up the Missouri in 1807 at the head of a 42-man trading and trapping expedition that included Corps of Discovery veteran George Drouillard among its members. This was the first large fur-trading party to depart from St. Louis with the intention of leaving behind the familiar region of the lower Missouri River and heading west into unexplored territory. En route Lisa recruited another veteran of the Lewis and Clark Expedition, John Colter, a particularly valuable addition to the party. Colter was returning from a winter trapping in the foothills of the Rockies, where he had gone with two independent fur traders, Forrest Hancock and Joseph Dixon.

The Lisa Expedition branched off from Lewis and Clark's path up the Missouri when its members reached the mouth of the Yellowstone River. They followed the Yellowstone west to the mouth of the Big Horn River. There they established a trading post called Fort Raymond. From Fort Raymond, John Colter went on alone to pass the word about the new trading post to surrounding Native American tribes. Colter crossed the Wind River Mountains in present-day Wyoming, the first American to explore that mountain range, which would figure largely in the story of western migration over the next half century. He viewed the Teton Mountains from a distance. In northwestern Wyoming, he came upon an incredible region of thermal hot springs and geysers, unlike anything any white explorer in the West had ever seen before. When Cody returned to Fort Raymond to report on what he had seen, no one believed him. His fellow trappers laughed at the tale of "Colter's Hell."

No one was laughing at Manuel Lisa when he returned to St. Louis the following spring, having turned a healthy profit on his venture up the Yellowstone. He had now emerged as the leading figure in St. Louis's fur-trading community and easily attracted partners, including the Chouteaus and William Clark, to invest in his newly organized St. Louis Missouri Fur Company. The enterprise, its name soon shortened to the Missouri Fur Company, sent out trappers and traders as far west as the Three Forks region of Montana. In a hostile encounter with Blackfeet Indians in summer 1808 near the Three Forks, another veteran of the Lewis and Clark Expedition named John Potts was killed, and John Colter barely escaped with his life. Captured by the Blackfeet, Colter was stripped naked and given a head start to escape by the Blackfeet warriors, who wanted to enjoy a little sport before killing him. To the Blackfeet's dismay, Colter managed to kill one of his pursuers and outrun the rest. After an epic seven-day flight through the wilderness, he arrived back to the safety of Fort Raymond.

While Lisa's employees in the Rockies were risking life and limb in the far West, Lisa himself was busy establishing a chain of trading posts, including Fort Manuel and Fort Lisa. He was distrusted for his sharp trading practices and disagreed with his partners in the Missouri Fur Company, which was dissolved in 1813. In 1819, he formed a new company of the same name, which he ran until his death in St. Louis in 1820. His sometime partners, sometime rivals, the Chouteaus, remained important figures in the fur trade for many more years, in a variety of companies, pushing beyond their traditional trade routes on the Missouri to the Rockies, until the decline of the fur trade in the 1860s led them to concentrate on other enterprises.

JOHN JACOB ASTOR'S FUR EMPIRE

St. Louis was not the only city where fortunes were made in the fur trade; New York City was another. There the great figure was John Jacob Astor. Born in Germany in 1763, Astor immigrated to the United States in 1783. He carried with him a supply of flutes to sell in his newly adopted homeland. Through a chance encounter with a fur merchant on the ship that carried him across the Atlantic, Astor decided furs would prove a more profitable business. A short, heavyset, and comfort-loving man who never shared the wilderness hardships of his employees, Astor nonetheless played a significant role in opening up the West.

Early in 1808, Astor wrote to Thomas Jefferson seeking the president's approval for a bold new trading venture. While Manuel Lisa was developing a trading empire that extended up the Missouri and the Yellowstone to the eastern edge of the Rockies, Astor wanted to proceed directly to the fur-rich Columbia River basin and open a permanent fur-trading post at the river's mouth. Lisa and the Chouteaus were operating their business in what was already, thanks to the Louisiana Purchase, territory considered part of the United States. Astor proposed opening up an outpost in the "Oregon Country." This was territory variously claimed by the British, the Spanish, and the Russians and to which, as yet, the United States had made no formal claim despite Lewis and Clark's recent exploit. Astor's enterprise, if successful, would strengthen the U.S. claim if and when the Americans decided to extend their nation's boundaries to the Pacific.

Jefferson was pleased with Astor's plans, as were the New York politicians Astor also approached for support. In April, Astor's American Fur Company was chartered by the New York state legislature. Later, Astor created the Pacific Fur Company, a branch of the American Fur Company, to concentrate on trade in the Northwest. Meanwhile in Canada, Astor's rivals heard of his plan and understood the threat it posed to their own commercial interests. He was also a threat to the British claim to the Oregon Territory.

By 1810, Astor was ready to make his move. He devised an intricate plan to send two expeditions to the mouth of the Columbia, one by sea and one by land, which would meet up and establish a trading outpost. To carry out the seaborne operation, Astor purchased a 94-foot (28-m) merchant vessel called the *Tonquin* and put it under the command of Jonathan Thorn, a U.S. Navy veteran. Loaded with more than $50,000 worth of trade goods and carrying a party of about 30 experienced fur traders, mostly French Canadians, the *Tonquin* set sail from New York Harbor on September 6, 1810.

At the age of 20, John Jacob Astor immigrated to America from Germany to sell flutes. He became a fur trader and the first multimillionaire in the United States.

Thorn proved a good sailor but a poor commander. He was soon involved in a hostile dispute with the fur traders onboard. He nearly abandoned 10 of them on a stop at the Falkland Islands, when they were late returning to the ship. He returned to pick them up only when the nephew of one of the men he had left behind put a pistol to his head.

The *Tonquin* finally reached the Columbia on March 22, 1811, six months after setting sail from New York. The river's mouth, with its notoriously treacherous sandbars and high waves, had already earned a reputation as "the graveyard of the Pacific." While the *Tonquin* sat at anchor offshore, Thorn ordered his first officer, John Fox, to take a longboat into the river to find a safe channel. The longboat and its crew disappeared without a trace. A second boat followed but it met disaster, and only two men were eventually found on shore. Thorn finally took the *Tonquin* into the river's mouth on his own. In a bay on the river's southern shore, at the site of present-day Astoria, Oregon, the expedition built Fort Astoria, a 90-foot-square (27-m-sq) stockade protected by four small cannons. It became the oldest permanent settlement founded by U.S. citizens west of the Rockies.

The Pacific Fur Company was now in business. Thorn set sail up the Pacific coast for Vancouver Island, where he heard there was rich fur trading. There he got into a quarrel with the local Salish Indians, several hundred of whom swarmed aboard the *Tonquin*. They killed Thorn and his crew. According to a somewhat suspect version of the end of the *Tonquin*, popularized by novelist and essayist Washington Irving, a dying crew member managed to blow up the ship's powder magazine, sinking the ship and avenging its crew with the mass death of the Salish boarders.

While Thorn and his ill-fated crew were carrying out Astor's seaborne plan, another party hired by Astor was on its way overland. The leader of the expedition was Wilson Price Hunt. Born in New Jersey in 1783, Hunt had moved to St. Louis in 1803. He had been among the St. Louis residents who cheered Lewis and Clark on their return in 1806. Astor hired him in 1809 to lead a party westward along the Lewis and Clark trail.

Before he set off, Hunt had long conversations with Lewis and Clark veteran John Colter, and perhaps with William Clark himself. He was convinced that Lewis and Clark's route was probably not the best one to follow. He believed that a more southerly route across the interior, following the Yellowstone rather than the Missouri River, offered a surer path to and over the Rocky Mountains. In October 1810, about a month after the *Tonquin* set sail from New York Harbor, Hunt and his party headed by boat a short way up the Missouri. At the mouth of the Nodaway River in present-day Andrews County, Missouri, they made their winter camp. Hunt returned downriver to St. Louis in January and recruited a dozen more travelers and an interpreter, Pierre Dorion, the son of an interpreter who had worked for Lewis and Clark. In March he set off again up the Missouri with 60 men along with Marie Dorion, wife of Pierre, and their two children.

Hunt's plans changed again in May. Meeting some experienced trappers en route, he was convinced by them that, rather than following the winding path of the Yellowstone River by boat, he would do better by striking off overland on horseback. Purchasing horses from the Arikara Indians, Hunt's party set off across the Dakota plains in July, following the Grand River westward. At first they made good progress, traveling through knee-high prairie grasses that kept their horses well fed while they feasted on buffalo. They traveled on a south-westerly angle that took them across a corner of present-day Montana into present-day Wyoming. By mid-August, they reached the Powder River range of mountains. They followed the Big Horn Mountains in September and then crossed the Continental Divide at Union Pass in the Wind River Mountains on September 16. Two weeks later, guided by friendly Shoshone, they crossed Teton Pass and came down into present-day Idaho to find a "beautiful plain," according to Hunt, full of antelope and wild cherries.

Hunt's opinion of the landscape soon changed, as they began the most difficult part of their journey. At a camp on the banks of the Snake River, they built dugout canoes from cottonwood trees, setting off downriver on October 19. They hoped to follow the Snake all the way to the Columbia. The river had seemed broad and inviting where they entered it, but it soon narrowed between high, rocky banks and grew rapid and treacherous. Boats were often swamped, one of the party drowned, and they lost precious supplies and time. Finally, on November 9, finding the river utterly impassable, Hunt split his party in two. One party proceeded up the south bank, while the other went on the north bank.

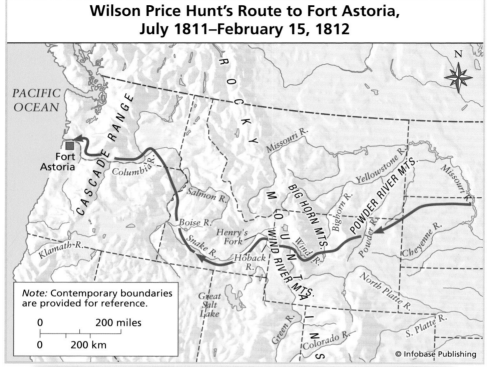

Wilson Price Hunt's Route to Fort Astoria, July 1811–February 15, 1812

Wilson Price Hunt was hired by John Jacob Astor to lead an expedition to the West Coast using information supplied by the Lewis and Clark Expedition. Hunt followed a more southerly route over the Rocky Mountains and actually beat Lewis and Clark's time by two months.

Rough terrain, snow, and hunger made them despair of ever reaching their goal. The two parties lost contact with each other and made their ways separately westward.

Finally, on January 21, Hunt's party reached the Columbia River. "With difficulty," Hunt noted in his journal, "I expressed the joy at the sight of this river."

Heading down the Columbia to its mouth, they met a Clatsop Indian who, Hunt noted, asked "for news about Mr. Lewis and Mr. Clark and some of their companions." On February 15, 1812, they reached Fort Astoria. Their companions who had left them at the Snake River had already arrived safely. "It was a great delight for travelers overcome with weariness to rest comfortably, surrounded by friends, after such a long journey in the midst of savage people of whom it is always wise to be wary," Hunt wrote of the occasion. Although they had chosen an impractical route across the continent, they had actually beaten Lewis and Clark's time traveling from St. Louis to the Pacific by two months.

THE WAR OF 1812 AND ITS AFTERMATH

The trading post the Astorians established on the Columbia River would strengthen U.S. claims to control of the Oregon Territory. But the U.S. flag did not fly very long over Fort Astoria before it was replaced by the British flag. Although the United States declared war on Great Britain four months after Wilson Price Hunt's party reached Fort Astoria, news of the War of 1812 did not reach the Astorians until January 1813. John Jacob Astor was worried about the future of his business and asked the U.S. government to send soldiers to the Pacific Northwest to defend Astoria. But the war was going badly in the East, and there were no soldiers to spare for such a distant and unimportant outpost.

Meanwhile, British fur traders saw their chance to eliminate a commercial rival. In October 1813, a party from the North West Company appeared at the gates of Fort Astoria, demanding that the trading post be sold to them upon the threat of an attack from the Royal Navy. Astor's employees, many of whom were Canadian-born and former employees of the North West Company themselves, had no particular interest in dying for John Jacob Astor or the United States. They knew it was wise not to resist, so they quickly agreed to sell the fort to the North West Company. It was renamed Fort George, in honor of George III. Most of Astor's employees now went to work for the North West Company.

With the peace settlement of 1814 calling for the return of all captured territory, Americans regained access to Oregon, although not to Fort Astoria, which remained in British hands. A separate treaty, known as the Treaty of 1818, essentially left the future of the Pacific Northwest up for grabs between the United States and Britain. Americans and British citizens alike were given the right to move freely, conduct business, and settle in the region stretching above the Spanish-controlled territory to the south in California and below the Russian-controlled territory to the north in Alaska.

Since 1810, the North West Company had maintained a trading post called Spokane House near present-day Spokane, Washington. In

1824, the Hudson's Bay Company established another trading post at Fort Vancouver (present-day Vancouver, Washington). From Fort Vancouver, for the next two decades, the Hudson's Bay Company's Columbia Department extended its fur gathering over an enormous stretch of future U.S. territory, including northern California, Oregon, Washington, Idaho, and Utah. By the time Americans came to control this region, the beavers would be all but wiped out. This overtrapping was a deliberate policy. British traders hoped that by creating a scarcity of furs, U.S. trappers would not bother to come to the Pacific Northwest if they knew that there were no furs to be taken there. If the trappers stayed away, so the thinking went, so would U.S. settlers.

THE SNAKE RIVER COUNTRY EXPEDITIONS

In the nineteenth century, the Snake River country was considered to be all the land drained by the Snake River, from southern Washington to northern Utah. Lewis and Clark had explored some of this territory on their westward journey in 1805 and their return in 1806. In the years that followed, traders from the North West Company made some brief forays into the region. The greatest explorer of the region was undoubtedly Peter Skene Ogden.

Ogden's father was an American Loyalist who fled to Canada in the aftermath of the American Revolution. Born in Quebec in 1794, Ogden grew up in Montreal, where he briefly worked for John Jacob Astor, who maintained a fur warehouse in the city. In 1809, he joined the North West Company. In fall 1810, the North West Company sent him on his first fur-trading mission westward, to Canada's Saskatchewan River region. He developed a reputation for violence, engaging in cruel pranks against his rivals and murdering a Native American in 1816 for trading with the Hudson's Bay Company. None of this seemed to bother his employers in the North West Company, who continued to give him more responsibility. In 1818, he traveled from a North West Company trading post at Île à la Crosse, across the Rockies and down the Columbia to Fort George (formerly Fort Astoria). For the next several years, he served at Fort George and the North West trading post Spokane House.

The North West and Hudson's Bay companies merged in March 1821. At first, the Hudson's Bay Company refused to employ Ogden.

After Ogden had made a trip to London to plead his case, in 1823, he was rehired to lead trading expeditions into Snake River country.

From his first expedition in 1824–1825, to his final expedition in 1829–1830, Ogden covered an astonishing amount of territory. He traveled all the way south through Nevada to the Gulf of California. He braved the extreme temperatures of the Mojave Desert as he crossed over to southern California. He visited unexplored regions of Oregon, Idaho, and Utah, returning across eastern Oregon home to Fort Vancouver. Ogden's expeditions were phenomenally successful in exploring new territory, yet he failed to create the "fur desert." U.S. trappers and settlers came to the region in larger and larger numbers.

On his return from his last and longest expedition, the Hudson's Bay Company sent him to the northwest coast of what would become British Columbia. Here he established a trading post near the mouth of the Nass River. Later he would be put in charge of a Hudson's Bay Company trading post at Fort Vancouver, and he died in Oregon City in 1854. His role in the exploration of the Snake River country is memorialized in the name of Utah's second-largest city, Ogden.

WILLIAM HENRY ASHLEY AND THE ROCKY MOUNTAIN FUR TRADE

While British and U.S. traders were competing in the Northwest, other U.S. fur traders were exploring the region of the southern Rocky Mountains. Here the key figure was a Missouri businessman and politician named William Henry Ashley. Born in Virginia in 1778, Ashley moved to St. Louis in 1808. A natural leader, he would dramatically expand and transform the fur-trading business. In 1822, in partnership with a former associate of Manuel Lisa named Andrew Henry, Ashley's newly founded Rocky Mountain Fur Company advertised for the services of a hundred "enterprising young men." Among the young men responding were some destined to achieve the status of legends in the Old West. They were known as "Ashley men."

Rather than follow the model of Lisa and Astor and build permanent trading outposts where Native Americans would bring furs to exchange for goods, Ashley equipped his own men as trappers and sent them out on horseback throughout the Rockies. This cut the Native Americans out of the business. It also changed the status of the mountain men.

AFRICAN AMERICANS IN THE WESTERN FUR TRADE

In recent years, the role of African Americans in the exploration of the western United States has gained new attention from historians and the public. York, a slave who accompanied the Lewis and Clark Expedition, is probably the best known of these black explorers. Less well known are the exploits of the African Americans, both slaves and free men, involved in the fur trade. Jim Beckwourth, who was the free son of a slave mother, accompanied William H. Ashley on one of his early trips up the Missouri. In later years, he prospered as an independent trader. By the end of his life, he was a rancher in California. Moses Harris, another of the black "Ashley men," later went on to guide wagon trains along the Oregon Trail. Peter Ranne, another free black, accompanied trapper Jedediah Smith through the Mojave Desert to California. African Americans were also employed at fur-trading posts as cooks, hunters, and blacksmiths.

No longer employees, they were now "free trappers," or what would today be called independent contractors. They brought in their year's harvest of furs to trade at an annual summer rendezvous, held at an agreed-upon time at one or another centrally located river valley. Each rendezvous, which involved several weeks of rowdy celebration as well as shrewd bargaining, proved a very successful way of doing business. After several profitable years, Ashley sold off his interests in the fur trade, leaving him free to carry on his political career. The free-trading rendezvous system Ashley established lived on for another decade and a half, the glory years of the Rocky Mountain fur trade.

JEDEDIAH SMITH

Perhaps the most famous of the Ashley men, and certainly the greatest explorer among them, was trapper Jedediah Smith. Born in Bainbridge, New York, in 1798, as a teenager he read the 1814 edition of the Lewis and Clark journals and was drawn to the West.

At age 22, he arrived in St. Louis and signed up as an Ashley man. There was something about him that inspired confidence among his fellow trappers, and Ashley decided to entrust Smith with the leadership of the next group of mountain men he sent west. Smith ably led a party across the Badlands and Black Hills of the Dakotas in 1823, spending that winter in the Wind River Valley. In spring 1824, he rediscovered South Pass in the Wind River Mountains, whose existence had been forgotten since Robert Stuart had first crossed it in 1812. Smith led the first party of U.S. citizens to cross the pass from east to west, a route soon to be followed by thousands of Oregon-bound settlers.

Ashley made Smith a partner in his fur-trading business, now known as Ashley & Smith. Smith's greatest expedition came in 1826. On August 7, he set out with a small party of men from a site near present-day Soda Springs, Idaho. He headed southwest of the Great Salt Lake across the length of present-day Utah on a route that took him through present-day Zion National Park. Eventually he reached the shores of the Colorado River, at a site near present-day Las Vegas, Nevada. Mojave Indians whom they met living along the Colorado told them of an old trail across the Mojave Desert that had once been used for the trade in seashells between coastal and inland Native Americans. The trail took them to a small Spanish settlement on the California coast, present-day Los Angeles. The desert trip had been hard, as Smith later wrote: "There for many days we had traveled weary hungry and thirsty drinking from springs that increased our thirst and looking in vain for a boundary of the interminable waste of sands." Smith and his party were the first U.S. citizens to make the overland journey to California.

The Spanish authorities in southern California were not welcoming, however. Smith soon headed north to the American River near Sacramento. He headed into the Sierra Nevada, the 400-mile- (643-km-) long mountain range that ran down the eastern side of the great fertile valley of central California. He was, as always, looking for beaver but also for a way to cross the mountains. He had heard that there was a river called the San Buenaventura that cut through the mountains and linked the Pacific to the Great Salt Lake. Smith searched in vain for the mythical river. Heavy winter snows blocked the passes through the mountains, preventing his party from heading east.

Then, in May 1827, Smith set out with just two men to see if he could find a way across the Sierra Nevada. They found a pass, later known as Ebbetts Pass, and got across. This was the first time the mountains had been crossed by whites. On the eastern side of the range, they were back in desert country (later known as the Great Basin). Their crossing of this desert was another first for white explorers. On June 27, 1827, they reached the Great Salt Lake. Smith's epic journey was among the most difficult in the history of North American exploration. Returning to California later that year to rejoin the men he had left behind, Smith and his party were attacked by Native Americans on two different occasions. Of the 18 men who had set out with him the previous year, only Smith and three others survived.

Smith would have other adventures, exploring as far north as the Canadian border. He reported on British strength in the Pacific Northwest to the U.S. secretary of war. His luck ran out on May 27, 1831, when he was attacked and killed by Comanche Indians en route to Santa Fe.

THE DECLINE OF THE FUR TRADE

The fur trappers' exploits were widely celebrated in their own lifetime. In the 1830s, novelist and historian Washington Irving wrote vivid and somewhat fanciful accounts of the founding of Astoria, as well as the adventures of Benjamin Louis Eulalie de Bonneville. Bonneville, a French immigrant and U.S. army officer, played a significant role in the exploration of the Rockies (among other achievements, he was the first to take wagons over the South Pass). Jim Bridger, Kit Carson, and others also caught the popular imagination. Those fantasy stories about lone, heroic white men bravely facing down the challenge of wild terrain, wild animals, and hostile Native Peoples established the guidelines by which Americans would think of the West for generations to come.

But it was getting harder and harder to catch beavers, as the animal's population along the Missouri, the Yellowstone, the Columbia, and even remote streams in the Rockies declined in the 1820s and 1830s. Fortunately for the few remaining beavers, felt hats went out of fashion in Europe in the 1830s, in favor of silk hats. A beaver pelt that would have sold for $5 on the London market in 1829 brought a mere 85 cents by 1846. So at the same time that beavers were harder and harder to catch, there was less and less reward for making the attempt. The mountain men drifted off to other occupations, and into legend, but not before having made a significant contribution to the exploration of the American West.

4

The Exploration of Western Canada

AMONG THE NATIONS OF THE WORLD TODAY, CANADA IS SECOND only to Russia in total land mass. Canada's boundaries enclose nearly 4 million square miles (6.4 million sq km), including inland waters, a vast region stretching more than 3,200 miles (5,149 km) in width from Newfoundland in the east to the Yukon Territory in the far northwest. However, Canada is also one of the least densely populated countries in the world, home to one-tenth the population of the United States.

The history of the exploration of North America by peoples of European origins began in Canadian territory. In the late tenth century, a few hardy Norsemen under the command of Leif Eriksson found their way across the stormy waters of the North Atlantic and established settlements they called Helluland (probably in present-day Labrador), Markland (probably in present-day Nova Scotia), and Vinland (either in present-day Newfoundland or northern New England). It was a Frenchman, Jacques Cartier, who found the key to opening the Canadian interior to its initial exploration by Europeans. He came across the Gulf of St. Lawrence in 1534 while searching the coastline for the Northwest Passage. Returning to the gulf the following year, he sailed up what he called "the river of Canada," the present-day St. Lawrence River.

In a series of expeditions in the early seventeenth century, Samuel de Champlain thoroughly explored the St. Lawrence and the surrounding region. In the name of the king of France, he claimed the territory that became known as Quebec and planted the first French settlements in the region. Champlain reached the shores of both Lake Huron and

Lake Ontario in 1615, the first time any of the Great Lakes had been glimpsed by Europeans. In the decades that followed, French fur traders and Catholic missionaries emerged as the most important figures in mapping the Canadian interior, pushing their way through the Great Lakes region and beyond. In 1673, Jesuit missionary Jacques Marquette and trader Louis Jolliet traveled down the Mississippi and discovered the mouth of the Missouri River. They were followed by the Jesuit-turned-merchant explorer René-Robert Cavelier, sieur de La Salle, who sailed down the Mississippi to its mouth in 1682 and claimed the entire river valley and all the land surrounding its tributaries for Louis XIV of France. Thus was founded the great Louisiana Territory, whose ultimate fate would be decided only 121 years later with its sale by Emperor Napoleon to the United States.

French explorers and geographers clung to the hope that somewhere on the North American continent there could be found a water route that led to the Pacific. The St. Lawrence River, they believed, represented the eastern portion of this Northwest Passage. Somewhere to the west, they theorized, was a great western sea. According to some, the western sea took the form of a great "salt lake" linked to the Pacific by a river running west through the Rocky Mountains. It was thought of as a western version of Hudson Bay, poking deep and directly into the interior of North America from the Pacific. Either way, all the explorers needed to do was to find the route that would take them from the St. Lawrence to the western sea's shores, and the Northwest Passage would belong to France. At first the French explorers and cartographers thought that the Great Lakes (known to them only by tales passed along by the Native Americans) was this sea. Later, when they reached the Great Lakes and found that the lakes offered no direct outlet to the Pacific, they simply shifted the imaginary sea's location farther west.

HUDSON'S BAY COMPANY AND WESTERN EXPLORATION

The French in Canada were spurred onward in their exploration of the interior by the knowledge that if they did not quickly lay claim to the western territory and its rich resources in furs, their English rivals would. The English had their own claims to a large share of Canadian territory, based on their exploration and control of Hudson Bay. This

The St. Lawrence River connects the Great Lakes to the Atlantic Ocean. Jacques Cartier had hopes of finding the Northwest Passage to Asia using the St. Lawrence but found that there was no link to the Pacific Ocean. Still, much of French claims to Canada such as Quebec City (*above, along the St. Lawrence River*) are based on Cartier's explorations.

region was known as Rupert's Land (named for Prince Rupert, cousin to England's ruler Charles II and the first governor of the Hudson's Bay Company). It theoretically included all lands draining into Hudson Bay, about 1.4 million square miles (2.2 million sq km), although the French had competing claims to much of the same region.

Fortunately for the French, the Hudson's Bay Company proved sluggish in exploring territory farther to the west. French fur merchants had built their trading empire by going directly to the Native Peoples, laden with trade goods, and returning to Montreal with bundles of pelts. The Hudson's Bay Company, in contrast, preferred to have the Native Peoples do the traveling and come visit its principal trading post, the York Factory (or Fort). Company employees ventured farther west only occasionally and did not linger long away from the security of their own trading posts. There were some exceptions, but the Hudson's Bay Company made no attempts to follow up on its achievements.

It was only in the last quarter of the eighteenth century that the Hudson's Bay Company finally realized it had to move westward or risk financial ruin. Thanks to the British victory in the French and Indian War in 1763, New France no longer existed in Canada. The British flag, known as the Union Jack, flew over Montreal. Ambitious British merchants were moving into that city and revitalizing the fur trade that had been disrupted by the war. Montreal fur companies, soon to unite as the North West Company, were expanding their chain of trading posts westward and coming to monopolize fur trading with western Native Americans. Ironically, Britain's victory in the war worked to undermine the economic prospects of the principal British fur company in Canada.

No longer could the Hudson's Bay Company sit and wait for furs to be brought to its long-established trading posts. In 1774, Samuel Hearne established Cumberland House, the company's first trading post west of the shores of Hudson Bay, on the northern shore of Lake Winnipeg. In 1800, Peter Fidler, the company's chief surveyor and mapmaker, established Chesterfield House at the confluence of the Red Deer River and the South Saskatchewan River.

THE NORTH WEST COMPANY AND WESTERN EXPLORATION

In the late eighteenth and early nineteenth century, explorers associated with the North West Company, the Hudson's Bay Company's principal rival, set the pace in western exploration. Alexander Mackenzie achieved the distinction of being the first European, and quite possibly the first human being, to cross the North American continent north of Mexico. Born in 1764, near Dunkeld, Scotland, Mackenzie came to New York with his parents as a child in 1774 and moved to Montreal in 1778. In 1785, he traveled west as a fur trader for Gregory McLeod and Company, a fur company that was soon to merge into the North West Company.

The North West Company's dominance of the Canadian fur trade in the early nineteenth century was based largely on its control of trading in the Athabasca region. Lake Athabasca, Canada's fourth-largest lake, is located in present-day Alberta and Saskatchewan. Not only were the shores of the Athabasca rich in fur-bearing animals, but the lake gave traders and explorers access to a new set of river systems reaching far into the western and northern interior of the continent. These include the Slave River, flowing north to Great Slave Lake in the present-day Northwest Territories, and the Peace River, flowing west toward the Rockies.

In June 1789, Mackenzie set off from Fort Chipewyn on the southern shore of Lake Athabasca, up the Slave River to the Great Slave Lake. From there he set out into unknown territory on the river that would bear his name, the Mackenzie. Unfortunately, he discovered that Peter Pond, a fur trader and the first European to reach the shores of Lake Athabasca, had been misinformed or misunderstood what he had been told by the Native Americans. Pond had been told that the river flowing out of Great Slave Lake would provide a quick and easy water route to the Pacific. The Mackenzie River flows north rather than west, and when Alexander Mackenzie reached its mouth in mid-July 1789, he found himself at a dead end. He was on the edge of the Arctic Ocean instead of the Pacific.

In May 1793, Mackenzie set off again into unexplored territory, this time proceeding on the Peace River, which flowed west from Lake Athabasca. The Peace River took him and nine companions to the eastern slopes of the Rockies. They found a low pass across the mountains, subsequently known as Peace River Pass, and crossed over. On the western side of the Rockies they took to water again, heading west on a river they knew as Tacouche Tesse. It would later be called the Fraser, and Mackenzie optimistically believed it to be the Columbia. When the river proved too challenging, Mackenzie's party set off overland, still heading west. Mackenzie and his companions returned to water when they came to the westward-flowing Bella Coola River. This river carried them to its outlet on the Pacific, just north of Vancouver Island. On a boulder along the shore, Mackenzie smeared a triumphant message in a mixture of vermilion and bear grease: "Alexander Mackenzie, from Canada by land, the twenty-second day of July, one thousand seven hundred and ninety three." Mackenzie's discoveries, linked with the detailed coastal surveys being conducted that same year by British admiral George Vancouver's Pacific expedition, allowed London mapmaker Aaron Arrowsmith to produce the first reasonably accurate map of Canada's boundaries.

On a boulder in British Columbia, Canada, Alexander Mackenzie wrote
a triumphant message: "Alex Mackenzie, from Canada by land, the 22nd
day of July 1793." He had just found the Pacific Ocean, becoming the first
European to successfully complete the transcontinental crossing to the
Pacific north of Mexico. Pictured, a man pretends to rewrite Mackenzie's
message.

DAVID THOMPSON

Mackenzie's 1793 route was too far north and involved too many stretches of overland travel through rough terrain. The North West Company assigned one of its best men, David Thompson, to find an alternative route. Thompson, born in London in 1770, began to work for the Hudson's Bay Company in 1785. In 1789, he broke his leg and spent a year recovering from the injury. It was a year he put to good use, learning surveying and celestial navigation, which gave him a degree of scientific training that distinguished him from most of his fellow fur traders. After his recovery, Thompson was sent by the Hudson's Bay Company to map northern Manitoba and Saskatchewan, including the upper course of the North Saskatchewan River. But, typically short-sighted, the Hudson's Bay Company kept giving Thompson mundane commercial tasks. Dissatisfied with the company's neglect of his special aptitude for scientific exploration, Thompson quit in 1797 and went to work for the North West Company.

Thompson's first assignment from his new employer was to survey the trade route from Lake Superior to Lake Winnipeg. That same year he traveled southwestward on the Assiniboine River. He crossed the plains to the Missouri River and returned to Canada via the upper reaches of the Mississippi River. Thompson not only accurately mapped the location of trading posts and Indian villages (including the Mandan-Hidatsa villages on the Missouri, where Lewis and Clark would stay seven years later), but he offered a survey of the geography and vegetation of the region through which he passed. (Meriwether Lewis studied Thompson's 1798 sketch of the Great Bend of the Missouri River before setting out on his expedition up the Missouri.) In 1799, Thompson headed farther west, exploring the route between the Churchill River and Lake Athabasca. In 1800, he journeyed to Rocky Mountain House, the North West Company's trading outpost along the North Saskatchewan River. He set out to the Rockies, hoping to find an easily accessible pass, but for the moment he was unsuccessful.

On June 25, 1807, he found a pass through the mountains that would later be named Howse Pass, about 80 miles (128 km) northeast of present-day Banff. Five days later, now on the west side of the Rockies, Thompson stumbled upon the Columbia River, at a site near

MACKENZIE INSPIRES LEWIS AND CLARK

In 1801, a London publisher brought out the first edition of Alexander Mackenzie's *Voyages from Montreal . . . through the Continent of North America, to the Frozen and Pacific Oceans*. Historian Donald Jackson has described this account of Mackenzie's 1789 and 1793 expeditions through western Canada as "the most important geographical work in [Thomas] Jefferson's possession." Jefferson had known of Mackenzie's success in reaching the Pacific since at least 1797, and he eagerly read Mackenzie's book when he received a copy of it in 1802.

In his book Mackenzie described the pass that led him across the Rockies as "a beaten path leading over a low ridge of land," a mere 3,000 feet (914 m) in elevation. From there it had taken him only a month to reach the Pacific Ocean. Mackenzie's description of his route reinforced Jefferson's belief that the Rockies were basically similar to the familiar Allegheny Mountains of the east, low in height, and within easy striking distance of the ocean.

Voyages from Montreal was a wake-up call to Jefferson. If Americans did not act quickly to find their own Northwest Passage, they might well find themselves forever shut out of the Pacific Northwest. His decision to order Meriwether Lewis to begin planning an expedition to the Pacific was directly inspired by Mackenzie's achievement. When they set out up the Missouri in 1804, Lewis and Clark carried with them the Arrowsmith map that showed Mackenzie's discoveries.

present-day Golden, British Columbia. He did not yet realize the momentous nature of his discovery. He named the river the Kootenay, and it would be another three years before he came to understand that this was indeed the water route he sought to the Pacific.

In 1809, David Thompson opened three new trading posts for the North West Company: Kullyspell House, in present-day Idaho; Salish House, in present-day Montana; and Spokane House, near present-day Spokane, Washington. Thompson claimed the region stretching from present-day northern Idaho to present-day Washington State in the name of Great Britain. On another of his Rocky Mountain crossings, in January 1811, he found an important new route across the Rockies, Athabasca Pass.

Thompson finally realized that the river he had discovered and named the Kootenay was actually the Columbia. Learning of John Jacob Astor's plans to found a trading post at the mouth of the Columbia, the North West Company dispatched Thompson down the river in a race to claim the river's mouth for its own trading post. Thompson set out at the end of June 1811 from a point near present-day Kettle Falls, Washington, heading downriver in a single canoe with three *voyageurs.* On July 9, he stood at the confluence of the Snake and Columbia rivers, where he nailed a note to a tree boldly declaring: "Know hereby that this country is claimed by Great Britain as part of its territories, and that the North West Company of Merchants from Canada, finding the factory for this people inconvenient for them, do hereby intend to erect a factory in this place for the commerce of the country around."

Thompson would have hammered a similar note on a tree when he reached the Columbia's mouth on July 14, 1811. He was the first European to traverse the river's length from its headwaters to its outlet and could take justifiable pride in the achievement. But as a trading venture, his journey proved a failure. Astor's men had arrived at the mouth of the Columbia first. All told, Thompson had covered more than 50,000 miles (80,467 km) in 14 years of active exploration on behalf of the North West Company. By the time Thompson returned to North West Company headquarters at Fort William, the War of 1812 had broken out. Fort Astoria would soon fall into the hands of the North West Company after all.

THE MERGER OF THE NORTH WEST COMPANY AND HUDSON'S BAY COMPANY

The rivalry between the North West and Hudson's Bay companies in Canada grew so heated that it turned into open warfare along the Red and Assiniboine rivers. The British government finally stepped in to pressure the companies to set aside their differences. In 1821, they merged, retaining the name Hudson's Bay Company. An act of the British Parliament extended the merged company's monopoly over the fur trade in Canada all the way to the shores of the Pacific.

Both the British government and the Hudson's Bay Company hoped that the eventual western boundaries of Canada would reach far below the 49th parallel (the dividing line between the United States and Canada between the Great Lakes and the Rockies) to take in some or all of the disputed Oregon Territory (the present-day states of Washington and Oregon). In a treaty signed in 1818, Britain and the United States agreed to share control of the territory for 10 years, and the compromise was extended by a new agreement in 1827. But just as John Jacob Astor's men had beaten David Thompson to the mouth of the Columbia in 1811, so U.S. settlers beat their Canadian counterparts to the Oregon Territory in the decades that followed. By 1844, U.S. presidential candidate James K. Polk raised the cry "Fifty-four forty or fight" as a campaign slogan, meaning that he hoped that the Oregon Territory well up into the future Canadian province of British Columbia would become part of the United States. As president of the United States in 1846, he settled for less. The United States secured control of the future states of Oregon and Washington, while accepting a northern border to its national territory that stretched the rest of the way from the Rockies to the Pacific along the 49th rather than the 54th parallel.

The Hudson's Bay Company, knowing it was about to lose its trading posts along the lower Columbia River, had been busy setting up trading posts farther north along the Pacific coast. Until then, this territory had been visited only sporadically by ship-borne fur traders. The northern Pacific department of the Hudson's Bay Company (known as the New Caledonia Department) established its headquarters at Fort Victoria on the southern tip of Vancouver Island in 1843. Vancouver became a British Crown colony in 1849, to stop further northern expansion of the United States after the Oregon Territory passed to U.S. control. Meanwhile, small bands of Hudson's Bay Company fur traders mapped the wilderness of the Canadian northwest, river by river, lake by lake, mountain range by mountain range, at considerable risk to their lives and those of the men who accompanied them.

CANADIAN NATIONALISM AND WESTERN EXPLORATION

The pursuit of the beaver, and the profits derived from trade in its fur, remained central to Canada's western exploration well into the mid-nineteenth century. Increasingly, Canadian nationalism also emerged as a motive for further exploration. In the nineteenth century, for the first time in Canada's history, settlers took their place alongside fur traders and missionaries on the westward-moving frontier.

At the start of the nineteenth century, Canada was less a nation than an assortment of loosely linked colonial possessions. The Canada Act of 1791, passed by British Parliament, divided Quebec in two. One half now consisted of Lower Canada, the region of majority French population along the lower St. Lawrence River. The other half, Upper Canada, was the region of majority British population, along the upper St. Lawrence River and the Great Lakes. Both Lower and Upper Canada had their own local governments, but both remained below the British Crown. To complicate matters, there were also crown colonies such as Newfoundland, royal provinces such as Nova Scotia and New Brunswick, plus the huge swath of Rupert's Land administered by the Hudson's Bay Company.

If anything can be said to have pushed Canada toward true national identity, it was the War of 1812, perceived by most Canadians as a war of aggression launched by the United States. The next half century saw a series of steps that created a unified nation. In 1840, the Act of Union passed by Parliament joined the provinces of Upper and Lower Canada under a single central government. And, in 1867, the British North America Act created the Dominion of Canada out of the provinces of New Brunswick, Nova Scotia, Ontario, and Quebec. The federal government consisted of an elected House of Commons and an appointed Senate that would make laws for the country as a whole. Canada now enjoyed self-rule in domestic affairs (it would not gain full independence in foreign affairs until 1931). The Parliament of the new Dominion of Canada met for the first time in November 1867 and selected John Alexander Macdonald as prime minister.

Macdonald, who would serve in office as prime minister almost continuously until his death in 1891, was determined to foster Canada's westward expansion. Under his leadership, the provinces of Manitoba and British Columbia joined the Canadian Confederation (as well as Prince Edward Island on the Atlantic coast). He also obtained the transfer of the territory from the Hudson's Bay Company to the Confederation of the Northwest Territories. To tie these new Canadian possessions together,

John A. Macdonald became the first prime minister of Canada in 1867. During his tenure, he expanded and united the country and was a big supporter of a national railway.

Macdonald encouraged the building of the Canadian Pacific Railway, which was under construction from 1882 to 1885. He also fostered further scientific exploration. In the early 1870s, government-sponsored surveyors set out to establish an accurate map of Canada's border with the United States and to survey the lands under federal administration in the Northwest Territories with the hope of attracting settlers.

All these efforts would have counted for little if it had not been for the choice made by tens of thousands of Canadians to move west. Until the middle of the nineteenth century, the number of whites in the Canadian West who did not make their livelihood from the fur trade was very small. That began to change with the discovery of gold in the West. With the construction of the Canadian Pacific Railway, wheat farmers and cattle ranchers began to move out onto the prairies. The arrival of a sizable number of Canadian settlers in the prairie provinces and along the Pacific coast meant that Canada had won its race with the United States. Like its neighbor to the south, it, too, would succeed in reaching "from sea to shining sea."

5

The U.S. Army Corps of Topographical Engineers

IN 1813, THE SECOND YEAR OF THE WAR OF 1812, CONGRESS authorized the creation of a unit of topographical engineers in the U.S. Army. Topography is the study of landscape features, both natural and human-made. Topographical engineers apply that study to solving practical problems, like planning where to build roads or railroads. Military topographical engineers address the questions that confront armies in the field. When Congress authorized the creation of the topographical engineers as a military unit, Congress specified that they were "to make such surveys . . . as the commanding generals shall direct; to make plans of all military positions which the army may occupy and of their respective vicinities, indicating the various roads, rivers, creeks, ravines, hills, woods, and villages to be found therein; [and] to accompany all reconnoitering parties sent out to obtain intelligence of the movements of the enemy or his positions."

When the War of 1812 ended, U.S. military forces were drastically reduced in size. The military soon found it had further need of the services of well-trained topographical engineers as it turned its attention to guarding the nation's expanding western frontiers, as well as its vulnerable coastlines. In 1816, Congress authorized the creation of the Topographical Engineers Bureau, under the command of the Office of Chief Engineer of the U.S. Army. The engineers of the Topographical Bureau—reorganized and renamed in 1838 as the Corps of Topographical Engineers—played a leading role in exploring and mapping the western United States.

ORIGINS OF THE LONG EXPEDITION

One of the most famous of the explorers who came from the ranks of the Topographical Engineers was Stephen Harriman Long. Born in Hopkinton, New Hampshire, in 1784, Long attended newly established Dartmouth College. With the coming of war in 1812, Long enlisted in the U.S. Army as a second lieutenant in the Corps of Engineers. At the end of the war he decided to stay on in the military and taught mathematics at the U.S. Military Academy at West Point. He transferred to the Topographical Engineers at the end of April 1816, shortly after Congress authorized the unit's creation. Long carried out some of the unit's first frontier assignments as he explored the Illinois, Fox, Wisconsin, upper Mississippi, and Minnesota rivers. His goal was to find sites for new forts.

In this 1862 Mathew Brady photograph, nine topographical engineers for the U.S. Army pose at their headquarters, near Yorktown, Virginia, during the Civil War. "Topogs" took part in military campaigns and aided in the development of canals, railroads, harbors, lighthouses, and roads.

In 1819, Major Long was given a new assignment. Colonel Henry W. Atkinson was leading 1,000 U.S. soldiers up the Missouri River in a show of force designed to impress both the Native Americans who lived along the river and the British in Canada. They were determined to establish full control over the upper Louisiana Territory. Atkinson's command, known as the Yellowstone Expedition, was carried up the Missouri in five steamboats, the first time that a large number of troops had been moved into potentially hostile territory by means of this new technological wonder. They hoped to reach the mouth of the Yellowstone before winter.

The War Department decided to send along a group of trained scientific observers. On May 5, 1819, almost 15 years to the day after the start of the Lewis and Clark Expedition, Major Long and other topographical engineers, scientists, and soldiers set off down the Ohio River from Pittsburgh. They traveled on the steamboat *Western Explorer.* They hoped to catch up with the rest of Atkinson's force on the Missouri.

Their trip received much publicity in newspapers. One article predicted that Long's party would "remedy the defects of the plan so boldly executed by Lewis and Clark" by advancing the cause of "universal science." Lewis and Clark had proved to be gifted observers of the natural world. But when their expedition set out in 1804, Lewis possessed only a smattering of scientific education and Clark none at all. In contrast, Long's expedition included three trained military topographers, including Long, Lieutenant James Graham, and West Point cadet William Swift. It also employed three civilian scientists: botanist William Baldwin, zoologist Thomas Say, and geologist Augustus Jessup. Two artists accompanied Long to bring back a record of the landscape, animals, plants, and Native Americans the expedition would encounter en route: the English-born Samuel Seymour and Titian Ramsay Peale, who was the son of the famed Philadelphia artist-naturalist museum-proprietor Charles Willson Peale.

Reporters wrote a vivid description of the departure of the steamboat, the *Western Explorer.* It made quite a spectacle: "The bow of this vessel," a St. Louis newspaper reported, "exhibits the form of a huge serpent, black and scaly, rising out of the water from under the boat, his head as high as the deck. . . ." From the serpent's open mouth the smoke of the steamboat's engines belched forth. The explorers hoped the smoke would scare off Native Americans. The steamboat was also equipped with a brass cannon and four brass howitzers. The men were supplied with muskets, rifles, and cutlasses.

In September, Long's group caught up with the main force under Colonel Atkinson. The Yellowstone Expedition had not been going well. Unlike the *Western Explorer*, the steamboats used by Atkinson's troops were poorly designed for the Missouri's shallow waters. They were soon abandoned. Instead of riding at their ease upriver, Atkinson's soldiers now had to march along the riverside. By the end of September 1819, the soldiers were weary and nowhere near the Yellowstone. They had only gone as far as Old Council Bluffs in present-day Nebraska. There they halted and built their winter camp. Long's men set up their own camp nearby.

Over the next few months, many of Atkinson's men died from disease and cold. Meanwhile, Major Long had returned to Washington. He reported to Secretary of War James C. Calhoun on the expedition's progress. While he was there, Calhoun decided to call off the Yellowstone Expedition. But the War Department gave Long's scientific unit a new assignment. Instead of following the Missouri to the mouth of the Yellowstone, as originally planned, Long was now ordered to take his party west along the Platte River. He was told to find its source in the Rocky Mountains. His group would then return east by way of the Arkansas and Red rivers.

Long rejoined his men at Council Bluffs on May 27, 1820, with their new orders. He was joined by Captain J.R. Bell as his second in command and Dr. Edwin. James replaced the departed William Baldwin as expedition botanist. On June 6, Long and 19 men set out on horseback with only a month's supply of food. When they came to a settlement known as the Grand Pawnee Village along the Wolf River, the Pawnee chief Long Hair commented on their bravery: "You must have long hearts to undertake such a journey with so weak a force, hearts that would reach from the earth to the heavens."

TO THE ROCKIES AND BACK

Just before sunset on June 14, Long's party reached the Platte River. The broad, shallow waters of the Platte have been described, with slight exaggeration, as 1,000 miles (1,609 km) long and only 6 inches

(0.5 feet) deep. The local Otoe Indian tribe called the Platte River "Nebraska," which means "flat water." Long and his men followed the river westward. On June 22, they came to the fork in the river. The North Platte leads toward present-day Wyoming. The South Platte goes toward present-day Colorado. They took the southern fork. On June 30, James wrote, "we left the encampment at our accustomed early hour, and at 8 o'clock were cheered by a distant view of the Rocky Mountains." By July 5, they had reached the site of present-day Denver, Colorado. They spied a high peak that they named Long's Peak.

Long's Peak was 14,255 feet (4,344 m) high. It is the highest summit in the Front Range of the Rockies. It remained unclimbed for the moment, but two other men from the expedition and Dr. James headed south. They climbed to the summit of Pike's Peak on July 14. Pike's Peak reaches a height of 14,110 feet (4,300 m). When the men climbed it, they had made to that date the highest recorded ascent of an American mountain north of Mexico. "From the summit of the Peak," James recorded, "the view towards the north, west, and southwest, is diversified with innumerable mountains, all white with snow. . . ." To the east they could see "the great plain, rising as it receded, until, in the distance, it appeared to mingle with the sky." James described nearby flowers, horned toads, and house finches. These descriptions were the first scientific record of the terrain, flora, and fauna of a 14,000-foot (4,267-m) mountain in North America. The explorers renamed the mountain James Peak. But that name did not stick. It is still known today as Pike's Peak.

James had glimpsed the headwaters of the Platte high in the Rockies. Long considered his task from the War Department completed. He did not lead his men into the mountains. Instead they headed south until they reached the upper Arkansas River. At that point, half the expedition headed east along the river under the command of Captain Bell. Bell and some of his men returned safely to Fort Smith in Arkansas, but along the way, three of the soldiers deserted. They took with them many of the expedition's scientific records, which were never found.

Long and the others continued south, searching for the Red River. They thought they had reached it when, on August 4, they came upon a river flowing out of the Rockies. They followed it east on a route that took them into the Texas Panhandle. They were the first Americans ever to travel through that region. But the river they were following was actually the Canadian, not the Red. They realized this when they found that, unlike the Red, it wound up emptying into the Arkansas River. On September 13, 1820, Long and his men reached Fort Smith in Arkansas.

Although the Long Expedition suffered from poor planning and geographical misjudgments, it made some significant contributions to popular and scientific knowledge. The two expedition artists, Samuel Seymour and Titian Ramsey Peale, created hundreds of valuable paintings and drawings. Seymour's paintings provided Americans with their first accurate depictions of the Rocky Mountain and Plains landscapes. Peale's works showed everything from prairie dogs to Native American buffalo hunters. His illustrations of Plains Indian tipis (teepees) shaped the American image of western Native American life. Dr. James's botanical collection, especially of alpine plants, also added to scientific knowledge of the West.

But the most lasting effect of the Long Expedition was to cement the popular belief that the region between the one hundredth meridian

Samuel Seymour was one of the artists to travel with Major Long on his expedition through the Great Plains. Seymour produced hundreds of paintings of the West and provided America with the first accurate depictions of frontier life. Above, this painting by Seymour shows Major Long holding a council meeting with the Oto (Missouri) Indians in 1819.

and the Rocky Mountains was a wasteland. Long called it the "Great American Desert." Long described the area through which he and his men had passed as "unfit for cultivation and of course uninhabitable by a people depending upon agriculture." The "scarcity of wood and water," he predicted, would "prove an insuperable obstacle in the way of settling the country." The name "Great American Desert" soon began appearing on maps of the region. Mapmakers used the same brown for other well-known deserts, like the Sahara in Africa.

In the decade following the Long Expedition, the army's topographers did little exploring but contributed greatly to the United States's economic development. The federal government encouraged internal improvements in the 1820s and 1830s, including the building of canals, railroads, harbors, lighthouses, and improved road systems. Major Long was assigned to survey the route along which the Baltimore and Ohio (B & O) Railroad laid its tracks. The topographers were also assigned to military campaigns, such as the conflict with the Seminole Indians in Florida in the 1830s.

JOHN C. FRÉMONT

Congress reorganized the Corps of Topographical Engineers in 1838. At the time, powerful political leaders believed that the federal government should encourage the exploration, settlement, and development of the western United States. The nation, they thought, should expand its borders whenever possible. This should be done even at the expense of other nations on the continent. The topographers would help the country do this. They were now an army corps. Their number increased to 36 officers. Nearly all of the "topogs" trained at West Point. One promising young lieutenant was John Charles Frémont.

Frémont was born in Savannah, Georgia, on January 21, 1813. By the time he was 17, Frémont was teaching mathematics in South Carolina. In 1833, he obtained a post as a civilian teacher of mathematics to midshipmen aboard the U.S. Navy ship *Natchez* and sailed on a long cruise off South America. Next, Frémont worked as a surveyor for the U.S. Corps of Topographical Engineers. He helped plan a railroad route between South Carolina and Ohio. Then he surveyed the boundaries of Cherokee Nation lands in western Georgia. Frémont would later write of this period, "I found the path I was 'destined to walk.' Through many of the years to come the occupation of my prime of life was to be among Indians and in waste [wild] places."

In 1838, the year of the reorganization and expansion of the Corps of Topographical Engineers, Frémont became a second lieutenant in the U.S. Army. He was assigned to the Corps of Topographical Engineers. Frémont explored the prairie region of the upper Mississippi Basin in present-day Minnesota. He worked as assistant to astronomer and explorer Joseph N. Nicollet. Nicollet had a lot to teach the young officer about geology, botany, and zoology. He also trained him in the practical skills necessary for managing a scientific expedition in the wilderness. "I could not dwell too much upon [Nicollet's] superb management of the expedition," Frémont later wrote in his memoirs, "not an article lost or broken throughout our long journey, not a horse injured or stolen, a set of the most ungovernable men in the world reduced in less than a week to perfect order & obedience." The following year, he continued with Nicollet on an expedition, traveling deep into the present-day states of North Dakota and South Dakota.

When Nicollet and Frémont returned to Washington, D.C., they worked on a map detailing their survey of the northern plains. Senator Thomas Hart Benton, who supported western expansion of the country, came to visit. It was a fateful meeting for Frémont. He courted Benton's beautiful 16-year-old daughter Jessie, and they were soon married. Senator Benton saw Frémont as the kind of explorer who could help him realize his dream of extending the United States to the Pacific.

With Benton's backing, Frémont was ordered on an expedition up the Kansas and Platte rivers in 1842. His task was to survey the trail along the banks of those waterways. He set off on horseback in early June, following the Kansas River. Frémont was in command of a motley crew of mountain men and *voyageurs*. They included the soon-to-be-famous scout Kit Carson and surveyor and cartographer Charles Preuss. Frémont led his expedition all the way to the Rockies. They crossed the South Pass and explored the Wind River Mountains.

Senator Benton hoped that Frémont's expedition would draw settlers to the South Pass and the Oregon Territory beyond. When he reached the Wind River Mountains in Wyoming, Frémont decided to climb a mountain that he called "Snow Peak." He mistakenly believed it was the highest in the Rockies. After days of struggling up the icy slopes of the mountain, he reached the summit on August 16. In a grand gesture, he planted a homemade U.S. flag at its summit. Senator Benton would later display his son-in-law's flag from the upper windows of his Washington, D.C., townhouse.

Frémont returned to Washington, D.C., at the end of October. He set to work on a report of his adventures. Written in the form of a daily journal, and published as a report to Congress, it caused a sensation. Its description of the ease of travel over the South Pass (which Frémont compared to climbing Capitol Hill in Washington, D.C.) and its thrilling account of the flag raising on "Snow Peak" did much to destroy the popular image that a vast wasteland barrier stood in the way of western migration. The report was reprinted in newspapers throughout the country and helped create "Oregon Fever." Thousands of settlers actually set off west along the Oregon Trail that year. Many Americans believed it was time to push the British trespassers out of Oregon Country once and for all.

THE MEXICAN WAR AND ITS AFTERMATH

When the United States went to war with Mexico in 1846, the Corps of Topographical Engineers joined the forces invading Mexican-held territory in the Southwest and California, as well as Mexico itself. Army captain Robert E. Lee was among the topographers who drew up maps for the U.S. military forces in Mexico. Lee later commanded the Confederate Army of Northern Virginia in the Civil War.

By September 1847 the U.S. flag was flying over Mexico City. Peace followed early the following year with the signing of the Treaty of Guadalupe Hidalgo on February 2, 1848. Mexico's northern border was set at the Rio Grande. The United States gained 525,000 square miles (844,905 sq km) of territory. These lands made up the future states of California, Arizona, Nevada, Utah, and parts of New Mexico, Colorado, and Wyoming. The United States annexed Texas and Oregon in the 1840s and purchased a strip of southwestern territory in 1853 in the Gadsden Purchase. The map of the United States came to assume the basic outline that is familiar today, with the exception of Alaska and Hawaii.

Victory brought new tasks for the Topographical Engineers. Topographer Major William H. Emory served with the U.S.-Mexico Boundary Commission. He helped map the country's new 1,800-mile (2,896 km) southern border. Over the next several years, Emory and his assistants gathered animal and plant specimens. They also studied archaeological sites, local Native American tribes, and the geology of the region.

In the decade and a half following the Mexican War, the Corps of Topographical Engineers conducted two dozen scientific surveys. Captain Howard Stansbury surveyed the Great Salt Lake in 1849. Lieutenant Joseph Christmas Ives explored the lower Colorado River in 1858. He reached the western edge of the Grand Canyon. The corps also surveyed potential routes for the proposed transcontinental railroad. The acquisition of California suddenly made this dream possible.

NATIVE AMERICANS AND THE CIVIL WAR

The officers of the Corps of Topographical Engineers were proud of their achievements. At least one of them, however, Gouverneur Kemble Warren, came to question the costs of U.S. expansion. He worried about its affect on the native peoples of western North America.

Warren was born January 8, 1830, in Cold Spring, New York. He graduated second in his class from West Point in 1850. That fall he became a second lieutenant with the Corps of Topographical Engineers. Warren spent most of his first year of active duty on the banks of the Mississippi, surveying its wandering course. He helped write a report recommending how to contain and channel the river's destructive power. After that he was assigned to the Pacific Railroad Survey.

In 1855, he joined a military unit commanded by General William S. Haney in the Dakotas. They hunted down a group of Brulé Sioux who had fought an earlier battle with the U.S. Army. On September 2, the unit found the Brulé Sioux at Blue Water Creek and attacked. This was Warren's first battle. The outnumbered Native Americans were driven from their encampment and killed in great numbers. It was not only Brulé warriors who died that day. Walking the battlefield afterward, Warren was shocked to find "women and children crying and moaning, horribly mangled by bullets." He wrote that he was "disgusted with the tales of valor" told by the soldiers in his own army.

In 1857, Warren was sent to the Black Hills of the Dakota Territory. In September, his party met with some Oglala Sioux. To the Sioux, the Black Hills were sacred. They were bitterly opposed to white settlement in the region. Warren insisted that he had to carry out his orders and

THE TRANSCONTINENTAL RAILROAD SURVEYS OF THE 1850S

In the early 1800s, the United States underwent a transportation revolution. In 1807, Robert Fulton built the first passenger steamboat, the *Clermont*. By 1811, steamboats were moving up and down the Mississippi River. The opening of the Erie Canal in 1825 connected New York City and the Great Lakes. It made it possible to speedily and cheaply move goods. By 1840, more than 3,000 miles (4,828 km) of canals were built. Most dramatically, between 1830 and 1840, nearly 3,000 miles of railroad track were laid. Railways allowed passengers and cargo to hurtle along at 25 miles (40 km) an hour. This was a speed previously unimaginable on land.

By the mid-1830s, politicians and railroad promoters had begun to dream of the day when a railroad line would stretch across the country. John C. Frémont led a privately funded expedition into the Rockies in 1848. He looked for a route for a transcontinental railroad. He did not find it. In 1853, Congress authorized four expeditions to search for a route for a transcontinental railroad. Officers from the Army Corps of Topographical Engineers led most of these expeditions in 1853–1854. Captain John Pope and Lieutenant John Parke led an expedition along the 32nd parallel. Lieutenant Andrew Whipple led an expedition along the 35th parallel. Captain George Gunnison led an expedition along the 38th parallel. (Parallels are mapmakers' lines, measuring latitude, or distance from the equator.) The northernmost expedition was led by Washington Territory governor Isaac I. Stevens. He explored a line from St. Paul, Minnesota, to Washington's Puget Sound.

The surveyors could not agree on a route for the first transcontinental railroad. However, the naturalists who joined the surveys learned enough about the regions to fill 17 volumes of official reports. It was not until the end of the U.S. Civil War that construction on the transcontinental railroad began, along the 42nd parallel. The iron rail link between the Atlantic and Pacific oceans was finally completed in 1869.

explore the hills. However, in his journal he agreed with the Sioux: "How true was all they said. The only security these indians can have in the possession of their country would be in its utter worthlessness to the whites."

In the end, the Sioux let Warren's party enter the Black Hills in peace. Warren carried out his mission and brought back to Washington, D.C., a great deal of information about the region's geology, flora, and fauna. He also made note of the region's economic potential. This included the existence of "valuable quantities" of gold in the Black Hills. After the Civil War, when gold was rediscovered in the Black Hills, the whites poured in. By 1877, Sioux claims to the Black Hills were no longer recognized by the U.S. government.

When the Civil War began in 1861, Warren and the other topographers gave up their peaceful exploring and surveying duties. Some, like Lieutenant Joseph Christmas Ives, joined the Confederate army. Others, such as New Hampshire native Stephen H. Long and New Yorker Gouverneur Warren, remained with the Union forces. Warren rose quickly through the ranks to become a general and chief engineer for the Army of the Potomac. The greatest moment of his military career came on July 2, 1863. On the second day of the Battle of Gettysburg, he noticed a rocky hill at the far left of the Union line. It was unoccupied. He gathered a force of defenders who held the hill in the face of repeated rebel attacks. The hill is now known as Little Round Top. General Warren's topographical instincts and quick action saved the Army of the Potomac from being outflanked and defeated at Gettysburg. Warren's actions contributed to the eventual triumph of the Union in the Civil War.

The Army Corps of Topographical Engineers did not survive the Civil War. In March 1863, it was merged with the Army Corps of Engineers. It lost its separate identity, thus ending a significant era in the history of the exploration of the West.

6

John C. Frémont and the Exploration of California

BEFORE CALIFORNIA WAS A NAME ON THE MAP, IT REPRESENTED A dream—a dream of wealth. In 1510, a Spanish author imagined an island in the New World "very near to the region of Earthly paradise." This island had gold so plentiful that even the "wild beasts" wore it as jewelry. The author called this imaginary place "California." In time, that name would be attached by Spanish cartographers to a long stretch of land along the Pacific coast of the North American continent. California would also come to be called the land of El Dorado—a legendary city of gold that the Spanish searched for but never found in Central America. California would indeed become a land of gold, first during the gold rush of 1848–1849, and then in later years when industry, agriculture, and natural resources made it the richest state of the United States. If California were a separate country today, it would rank among the top 10 nations in the world in terms of goods and services produced.

When U.S. politicians first began to talk about their nation's "Manifest Destiny" to spread from coast to coast, they looked to the Oregon Country as the key to unlocking the riches of the Pacific. Senator Thomas Hart Benton relished the days to come when "a stream of Asiatic commerce [pours] into the valley of the Mississippi through the channel of Oregon." But in the course of the 1840s, California replaced Oregon in the minds of many Americans, including Senator Benton, as the most desirable territorial prize to be won on the Pacific. Benton's explorer son-in-law, John C. Frémont, popularly known as "the Pathfinder," played a major role in the events that made that dream a reality.

EARLY CALIFORNIA EXPLORATION

The first European explorers to visit California saw little more than its shoreline. In 1542, Spanish explorer Juan Rodríguez Cabrillo sailed up the California coast in search of the Northwest Passage, making landfall at the sites of present-day San Diego and Santa Barbara. He traveled as far north as the site of present-day San Francisco, though he failed to discover San Francisco Bay. After Cabrillo died at sea, his second in command, Bartolomé Ferrelo, traveled even farther north in 1543. He reached an area near the present-day California-Oregon border. The English were next to arrive. Sir Francis Drake had raided Spanish towns and ships on the South and Central American coasts in his famous privateering ship the *Golden Hind* and came looking for a place to hide out and refit for the trip back to England. He made landfall north of San

In an 1849 Currier & Ives lithograph, men with picks and shovels coming from many directions and using methods of travel ranging from swimming to parachuting from an airship crowd onto a ship departing for California. This drawing depicts the excitement caused by the discovery of gold in the West and the resulting mass migration.

Francisco in 1579. Drake named the region New Albion and claimed it for Queen Elizabeth, a claim that did not stick. In the middle of the eighteenth century, the first Spanish settlements were created in California. Starting in 1769 and during the next half century, Franciscan missionaries established 21 missions in a coastal band stretching from San Diego to Sonoma. In 1776, the Spanish built a presidio, or fort, on San Francisco Bay. The settlement that grew up around the fort would be known until 1847 as Yerba Buena. All told, there were only a few thousand Spanish settlers in California by the start of the nineteenth century, and they showed little interest in exploring the lands that lay to the east of California's coastline.

THE ERA OF MEXICAN RULE

When Mexico gained its independence from Spain in 1821, California passed from Spanish to Mexican control. The Mexican government broke up the mission system, transferring church-owned lands to private hands as a way of encouraging Mexicans to settle in the region. The Mexican government worried that outsiders would rob Mexico of its northernmost province, and with good reason.

U.S. trading ships began to appear off the coast of California in the 1790s and brought back reports to the East of the beauty and the potential wealth of the region. Henry Richard Dana, who journeyed to California aboard a U.S. merchant ship in 1834 and described his adventures at sea in a widely read memoir, *Two Years Before the Mast*, thought the Mexicans had done little to exploit the riches of their province: "In the hands of an enterprising people," he wrote enviously, "what a country [California] might be!" The first American to reach California overland was mountain man Jedediah Smith, who arrived in 1826. Smith and other fur traders did not stay long, but in 1841, a group of U.S. settlers arrived, led overland by John Bidwell and John Bartleson. Swiss-born John Sutter also came to settle in California, building a trading post at the site of present-day Sacramento. Sutter's Fort became a way station in the early 1840s for U.S. settlers moving to California. Both the Mexican authorities and the U.S. settlers in California were well aware of what Texas had done in 1836, when Americans had overthrown Mexican rule and established their own independent republic. It would not be long before U.S. settlers in

California began hatching their own plans for challenging the Mexican government.

FRÉMONT'S 1843–1844 EXPEDITION

In March 1843, Lieutenant John C. Frémont of the U.S. Army Corps of Topographical Engineers was in Washington, D.C. He had just finished writing up the report of his 1842 expedition to the Rockies, which would later make him a popular hero in the United States. Now he was to return to the West, crossing the Rockies, to survey the trail to the Oregon Country. His father-in-law, Senator Thomas Hart Benton, backed the expedition in hopes that it would encourage more Americans to move to Oregon. Frémont's group would be well armed. He requisitioned a cannon and 500 pounds of ammunition, a heavy load to haul over the Rockies. Colonel John J. Abert, commander of the Corps of Topographical Engineers, was astonished to learn of the cannon. He wrote that Frémont was supposed to be leading "a peaceable expedition . . . an expedition to gather scientific knowledge." Frémont, knowing he had powerful friends to back him up if need be, took the cannon anyway.

At the end of May 1843, Frémont set off across the Kansas plains with 39 men on horseback and the cannon in tow. He hoped to find a route over the Rockies to the south of the now well-established South Pass route. At the trading post at Pueblo, Colorado, Frémont met an old trail companion, Kit Carson, whom he recruited on the spot to accompany the expedition westward. Frémont divided his party, taking 15 men up the Cache la Poudre River canyon in search of the new pass across the Rockies. He sent the others with the expedition's wagons and the bulk of their supplies over South Pass. The Cache la Poudre route proved too difficult, however, and, within days, Frémont's party headed north across the Laramie Plain to rejoin the others crossing the South Pass.

Once across the Rockies, Frémont suddenly decided to make a detour to the Great Salt Lake. Perhaps it was not so sudden, for he had brought along an 18-foot-long (5-m-long) experimental rubber boat with the expedition's supplies. It was "a frail batteau of gum-cloth distended with air, and with pasted seams," as Frémont described it. Thanks to visits by U.S. and Canadian mountain men, the Great Salt

Lake's location was already well known. Still, Frémont was the first to pronounce it a good place for settlers to come, surrounded by what he called "fertile and timbered" land. This description would influence the decision by Mormon settlers to migrate to Utah a few years later.

By the time he was en route again to Oregon, the weather was turning cold. Frémont gave his men the choice of whether they wanted to accompany the expedition any farther, and 11 chose to return to St. Louis. Frémont's reduced party then headed up the Snake River Canyon toward the Columbia.

THE GREAT BASIN

Frémont had his limits as an expedition leader. He was a poor planner, given to rash decisions and eager for glory, even if it came at the expense of carrying out his assigned duties. Nonetheless, he had one great strength as an explorer. He could look at a landscape and make sense of it. En route from the Great Salt Lake to Oregon, he had a geographical revelation. Between the Sierra Nevada of California to the west and the Wasatch Range of central Utah to the east, Frémont knew there lay a vast arid region. It was watered by a few rivers flowing down from those mountains, but where, he wondered, did the water go? He realized the region was the only place in the United States where, as he would write, the waters flowing down the mountainsides "have no connexion with the ocean, or the great rivers which flow into it." Frémont called this the "Great Basin," the name by which the region continues to be known today. The Great Basin includes most of present-day Nevada, as well as portions of western Utah, southern Oregon, and eastern California.

By late October, Frémont's party had reached the Columbia River and followed its south bank downriver. Frémont passed by several Hudson's Bay Company trading posts, symbols of British power in the Oregon Country that he found disappointing. But the British sent fur traders, not settlers, to the region. Frémont was encouraged by the number of recently arrived Americans he encountered along the way.

THE SIERRA NEVADA

On November 25, Frémont's party headed south from the Columbia along the side of the Deschutes River. They crossed the Klamath River and passed southeast of Upper Klamath Lake in southern Oregon. If

Frémont kept heading south, he would leave the Oregon Country and cross over into California. Frémont had now carried out his original assignment of scouting the Oregon Trail. His orders said nothing about continuing his exploration into California, which was, after all, foreign territory. But in another hasty decision, he decided to lead his men across the Sierra Nevada into the Mexican province.

The Sierra Nevada lie to the east of California's Central Valley, running 400 miles (643 km) on a north-south axis. They constitute the longest continuous mountain range in the United States. This includes such notable features as the granite cliffs of Yosemite Valley on the range's western slope and the towering peak of Mount Whitney, at 14,495 feet (4,418 m) the highest mountain in the United States south of Alaska. In a "Geographical Memoir" of his travels in California published in 1848, Frémont again displayed his gift for explaining landscape in his description of the Sierra Nevada's impact on California's climate: "[T]his great mountain wall receives the warm winds, charged with vapor, which sweep across the Pacific Ocean, precipitates their accumulated moisture in fertilizing rains and snows upon its western flank, and leaves cold and dry winds to pass on to the east. Hence the characteristic differences of the two regions—mildness, fertility, and a superb vegetable kingdom on one side, comparative barrenness and cold on the other."

Frémont and his men were heading south beside the barren, cold eastern slope of the Sierra Nevada, on a path that roughly followed the present-day California-Nevada border. Frémont got as far south as Lake Tahoe. It was now late January, far from the best time to attempt a mountain crossing. But Frémont had decided to cross the mountains and head to Sutter's Fort to buy supplies. Local Native Americans whom Frémont attempted to hire as guides across the mountains were astonished at Frémont's folly: "They looked at the reward we offered," he would later write, "and conferred with each other, but pointed to the snow on the mountain, and drew their hands across their necks, and raised them above their heads, to show the depth; and signified that it was impossible for us to get through." Although Jedediah Smith had crossed the mountain range in 1827, there had been no recorded crossing of the mountains in winter. Frémont could not be deterred.

They started up the mountain slopes on January 29. One thing soon became apparent. They were not going to get Frémont's cannon across the mountain and had to leave it behind. It took them a full month to fight their way through the deep snow in the mountains. Their Native American guides deserted them, and they had to kill off their horses one by one for food. Still they made it, passing over 9,338-foot (2,846-m) Carson Pass, later to become the major overland route for gold-seeking prospectors coming from the East. When they descended the western slopes of the Sierra Nevada into the valley below, they were, as Kit Carson later recalled with slight exaggeration, "naked and in as poor condition as men possibly could be."

THE GREAT VALLEY

The Central or Great Valley of California extends 450 miles (724 km) through the California interior. The valley is bounded on the north by the southern Cascades and the Trinity mountains and on the south by the Tehachapi Mountains. The valley was formed by two major river systems, the Sacramento to the north and the San Joaquin to the south. It was destined to become one of the world's richest agricultural regions.

Frémont and his men followed the American River down from the mountains to Sutter's Fort, where they rested and resupplied. On March 24, they rode south along the San Joaquin River. In mid-April, Frémont and his men left California, crossing a pass in the Tehachapi Mountains. From there they descended into Frémont's "Great Basin," reaching the site of present-day Las Vegas on May 3. Four months later, they were back in St. Louis, having traveled the last stretch down the Missouri by steamboat. They had been gone 15 months.

Settling back in Washington, Frémont sat down to write another narrative of his adventures. Congress ordered 10,000 copies, and more soon rolled off the presses in private editions. In his absence, Frémont had become a celebrity explorer, his deeds compared to those of Lewis and Clark. The maps Frémont produced with surveyor Charles Preuss were widely circulated. A few years later, returning east from yet another expedition, he had the great pleasure, as he wrote to a friend, of encountering "many strong and warm friends" among the settlers heading west. "They were using my maps on the road," he wrote proudly, "and you may judge how gratified I was to find that they found them perfectly correct. . . ."

FRÉMONT'S 1845–1846 EXPEDITION

While he was polishing his report, Frémont (now promoted to captain) received new orders from his Topographical Corps commander, Colonel Abert. He was to lead a third expedition west, this time to explore the headwaters of the Arkansas and Red rivers in the Rockies. The orders were issued at a moment of growing tension between the United States and Mexico over the future of Texas—and perhaps of the entire Southwest and Pacific coast. A new expansionist-minded president, James K. Polk, was about to take office. Congress passed a joint resolution calling

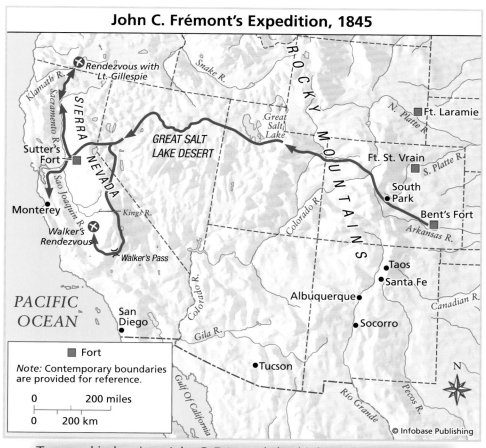

Topographical engineer John C. Frémont led a third expedition in 1845, this time to map the source of the Arkansas and Red rivers in the Rockies. Against official orders he went to California, nearly causing a war on Gavilan Peak, overlooking Monterey.

for the annexation of Texas, knowing full well that the Mexican government would be against it.

In early June, Frémont set out from St. Louis heading west to Bent's Fort, a fur-trading post on the Arkansas River in Colorado. Frémont sent part of his party, under command of Lieutenant James Abert (the son of Colonel Abert), to explore the Canadian River to its junction with the Arkansas. The bulk of the party, 60 men including Kit Carson, remained with Frémont. On August 16, they set off, following the Arkansas River westward. By mid-October, they were at the Great Salt Lake, where they spent two weeks exploring its shores. They pushed on into the Great Basin, crossing the Great Salt Lake Desert.

CROSSING THE SIERRA NEVADA AGAIN

On November 29, with 15 men, Frémont set out to find a new pass through the Sierra Nevada. Meanwhile, the larger party, under the command of veteran mountain man Joseph Walker took a more southerly route to climb an already known pass across the mountains. This was the same Joseph Walker who, back in 1833, had crossed the Sierra and glimpsed Yosemite Valley.

On December 4, Frémont and his men crossed the Sierras by a new route, a 7,200-foot (2,194-m) pass. Theirs was a relatively easy crossing under clear skies. A party attempting the same pass in 1846 would not be as lucky. A group of settlers led by Jacob and George Donner would be trapped in the mountains by winter storms and would descend into a nightmare of starvation and cannibalism before a remnant of the party was rescued. The pass was thereafter known as Donner Pass.

Descending to the sheltered western slope, Frémont's party enjoyed fine weather and warm temperatures. "We had made good our passage of the mountain," Frémont would later write, "and entered now among the grand vegetation of the California Valley." From there they had an easy ride to Sutter's Fort. After buying cattle and other supplies from Sutter, they headed south down the San Joaquin Valley in mid-December to rendezvous in the Sierras with the Walker party. Frémont's earlier decision to split his party proved to be a mistake. Frémont's party fought with hostile Native Peoples, and when they reached the King River, the scheduled rendezvous site in the Sierras, Walker's party failed to show up. Facing blizzards in the mountains, they retreated to the comforts of Sutter's Fort, arriving on January 15, 1846.

FRÉMONT'S MYSTERIOUS BEHAVIOR

Frémont's actions during the next six months are difficult to account for. They seem like those of a man waiting for something to happen. He wandered up and down the California coast and central valley. Sometimes he invited trouble; sometimes he avoided it. Sometimes he explored, but mostly he rode around with his heavily armed band of men. In mid-January, he took a few men down to the port of Yerba Buena (present-day San Francisco). He coined a name for the opening in the coastal mountains that lets the ocean into San Francisco Bay, calling it the "Golden Gate."

In San Jose, Frémont finally reunited with the remainder of his detachment under Joseph Walker, who had had a long and difficult passage over the mountains. Frémont spent some time exploring the coastal range near present-day Santa Cruz, California. There he came across the first redwood trees he had ever seen, the tallest living things on Earth. He was amazed to find trees of "a diameter of nine or ten feet" and reaching 200 feet (60 m) or higher into the sky. While Frémont was enjoying the "invigorating salt breeze" that blew in from the ocean, however, Mexican officials were growing more concerned about this large, well-armed band of foreigners riding at will through their countryside. Frémont had told the Mexicans when he rode through Monterey he was there only to gather supplies for a trip north to the Oregon Country. Now he headed south, past Monterey, and into the lower San Joaquin Valley.

CONFRONTATION WITH THE MEXICANS

The Mexican authorities finally decided they had had enough of John C. Frémont. General Don José Castro, the commander of the Mexican forces in California, sent him a letter by courier. It arrived in Frémont's camp on March 3. Castro ordered Frémont and his men to leave California immediately.

Frémont's response was to prepare for war. He moved his camp to a strong defensive position atop a coastal mountain called Gavilan Peak, overlooking the road to Monterey, where he had his men build wooden barricades. He had his men raise the U.S. flag on the hilltop. Mexican foot soldiers and cavalry gathered below. Then Frémont seemed to develop second thoughts about the impending battle. On the Americans' third day in their mountaintop fortress, their flagpole fell over. Frémont took that as a sign that he "had remained as long as the occasion required." Under cover of darkness on the night of March 9, Frémont pulled his men off the peak and set off again for Sutter's Fort.

Having backed down from fighting the Mexicans, Frémont instead launched an attack on a Native American village, an attack that Kit Carson, never known to shrink from a fight, referred to as "a perfect butchery." Frémont justified the assault on the Native Americans as vengeance for previous attacks on U.S. settlers, though in a Mexican province, protection of settlers would seem to have been a task for the Mexican army to carry out. Frémont's actions may have been intended to signal to the U.S. settlers that the U.S. Army was now on hand to back them up in any fight they might choose—with Native Americans or with Mexicans.

Frémont and his men returned to exploring in early April, heading north past Mount Shasta and crossing over into the Oregon Country. But as his men rode north, war was breaking out to the south. U.S. Army general Zachary Taylor led his forces into disputed territory near the Rio Grande, provoking a Mexican attack. This prompted a U.S. declaration of war. Meanwhile in California, small groups of settlers were preparing to take up arms against Mexican authorities, heartened by Frémont's mountaintop defiance of General Castro. But the U.S. settlers were puzzled by Frémont's disappearance at just the moment when they most needed his assistance. John Sutter later commented, "Flitting about the country with an armed body of men [Frémont] was regarded with suspicion by everybody." Historians are still divided about Frémont's real motives and strategy. What seems most probable is that he was simply undecided as to how far he could or should go in provoking California's Mexican rulers and was awaiting new orders or developments.

THE U.S. ANNEXATION OF CALIFORNIA

The turning point for Frémont came on May 9, when Archibald Gillespie from Washington, D.C., caught up with Frémont at Oregon's Upper Klamath Lake. He was carrying confidential orders, as well as the news of the outbreak of the war with Mexico. "The mission on which I had been originally sent to the West was a peaceful one," Frémont would write in his memoirs. But his new orders cleared him from his original duties as an explorer. Instead, "I was left to my duty as an officer of the American Army. . . ." The exact nature of the instructions Frémont received remains a mystery, but he interpreted them as giving him the go-ahead to seize California for the United States. "I saw the way opening clear before me. War with Mexico was inevitable; and a grand opportunity now presented itself to realize in their fullest extent the far-sighted views of Senator Benton, and make the Pacific Ocean the western boundary of the United States."

After some skirmishes with Klamath Indians, in which three members of Frémont's expedition were killed, they returned to the Sacramento Valley. There they found armed U.S. settlers preparing to attack Mexican forces in Sonoma. The rebels had adopted a flag bearing the words "California Republic" and a picture of a grizzly bear. The uprising became known as the Bear Flag Rebellion. Frémont would later claim a large share of the glory for the rebellion's success. He actually played only a minor role in fighting the Mexicans. But his presence in California encouraged U.S. settlers to believe that they could overthrow Mexican rule with the backing of their own government, so he does deserve some of the credit for what was to come.

Some of Frémont's men marched off to Sonoma with the settlers. He did not go with them, instead riding with 12 men to Yerba Buena (San Francisco), where they found no Mexican soldiers. Unopposed, they spiked the old Spanish cannons at the presidio guarding the entrance to the bay. Then he rode on to Sonoma. At a meeting of the Bear Flag rebels on July 5, he was chosen as the rebellion's leader.

Other U.S. military forces were beginning to arrive in California. The first of the newcomers came by sea. Commodore John Drake Sloat, commander of the U.S. Navy's small Pacific fleet, seized Monterey on July 7 and proclaimed California "a portion of the United States." Frémont's followers from his topographical party, as well as the rebellious settlers, were sworn into the U.S. Army as the "California Battalion." They were carried aboard a U.S. warship south along the coast to the Mexican-controlled port of San Diego, which was captured without opposition on July 29.

John C. Frémont became the leader of the rebels who seized the Mexican fort at Sonoma, claiming California as an independent republic. Here, he raises a flag featuring a red star and bear and the words "California Republic" in 1846.

Commodore Sloat now stepped down from command due to ill health. The new commander of U.S. forces in California, Commodore Robert F. Stockton, ordered Frémont to march north to aid in the capture of Los Angeles, which was taken without resistance. Commodore Stockton appointed Frémont military commandant of California. Soon after, the first serious resistance to the Americans took shape, with Mexican forces retaking Los Angeles and beating off U.S. counterattacks.

Frémont led his men back to Los Angeles in December, but they arrived too late to take part in the city's recapture. The hero of the battle was General Stephen Watts Kearny, a hard-bitten veteran of the War of 1812. Kearny and Stockton's combined forces defeated the Mexicans at a battle on the San Gabriel River on January 8–9, 1847. In doing so, they secured control of California for the United States.

Kearny considered himself the supreme U.S. military commander in California. Frémont, however, disagreed. Their feud turned nasty, and Kearny eventually brought charges against Captain Frémont for insubordination and mutiny. Frémont, in his own mind the hero of the California rebellion, returned to Washington, D.C., under arrest. He was court-martialed and found guilty, then dismissed from the army. President Polk offered to restore him to active duty in recognition of past service, but Frémont, angry and humiliated, refused the offer and resigned his commission.

FRÉMONT'S 1848 EXPEDITION AND HIS LATER CAREER

Though out of the army, Frémont remained an explorer. With Senator Benton's backing he headed west again in October 1848, on his fourth Rocky Mountain expedition. This time he searched for a possible route for a transcontinental railroad. The expedition's late start meant they would be arriving at the Colorado Rockies in the dead of winter. Frémont ignored warnings from experienced mountain men that the winter was shaping up to be one of the coldest they could remember. The expedition headed into the mountains and then was trapped by blizzards that left snowdrifts as deep as 25 feet (7 m). Frémont had been lucky in his winter crossings of the Sierra Nevada. This was the expedition on which his luck ran out. Ten of his men died of exposure and starvation. Conditions had been so bad that one of the corpses found by a rescue party showed signs of cannibalism.

Despite the court-martial that brought his army career to a dead-end, and despite the ill-fated 1848 expedition, Frémont's reputation as a hero of western exploration remained untarnished. In the popular mind, no other American was more closely linked to the acquisition of California than Frémont. When gold was discovered in 1848 at Sutter's Mill, in the foothills of the Sierra Nevada, Frémont's achievements were magnified a thousandfold. Tens of thousands of Americans flooded into California the next year over paths and passes that Frémont had explored, described, and mapped. Until 1848, the wealth of the West had been represented mostly by the profits from the fur trade, which was now in steep decline. After 1848, it would be gold, and later silver, and still later oil, that measured the region's importance to the U.S. economy.

Frémont himself became a wealthy man from the gold strike, since he had previously bought land on the slopes of the Sierra Nevada where gold was found. California had enough U.S. citizens to become a state in 1850, and Frémont was elected one of its two new U.S. senators. His writings remained as popular as ever; his *Report of the Exploring Expeditions to the Rocky Mountains in 1842 and to Oregon and North California in the Years 1843–44* went through 25 published editions in the United States and Britain in the decade following its 1845 publication. A popular American magazine in 1850 described Frémont as one of the three greatest figures in U.S. history, along with Christopher Columbus and George Washington.

Frémont made one final expedition in 1853–1854, again searching for a transcontinental railroad route. Increasingly he became known as a politician rather than an explorer. Frémont also became recognized in the 1850s for his opposition to slavery. In 1856, he accepted the presidential nomination of the newly organized Republican Party. He ran on the slogan "Free Soil, Free Men, Frémont," but he lost in November to Democrat James Buchanan. In 1860, with Abraham Lincoln as their candidate, the Republicans were victorious. When 11 Southern states responded by attempting to secede from the Union, Frémont quickly rejoined the U.S. Army and was promoted to general.

He proved as impulsive as ever. As Union military commander in Missouri in summer 1861, he issued an order freeing the slaves of rebellious slave owners in the state. President Lincoln immediately countered Frémont's order and dismissed him from the army, though less than two years later, Lincoln would issue his own, far broader, emancipation proclamation.

LEGACY OF THE PATHFINDER

In later years, Frémont struggled to stay afloat financially. His fortune had been eaten up by poor investment decisions and lawsuits. His days as an explorer were over, and not just because he was growing too old for the struggles of life on the trail. Exploration was changing. Frémont's way of exploring was becoming a thing of the past. The next wave of exploration in California would be done according to scientific norms and bureaucratic rules and regulations.

Most historical accounts of Frémont's career since then have dwelt on his many flaws as an expedition leader. His real achievements should not be minimized. Between 1842 and 1854, Frémont traveled more than 20,000 miles (32,186 km) on five expeditions. He made a significant contribution to geographical knowledge, dispelling the myth of the San Buenaventura River and identifying and naming the Great Basin. His writings and maps induced many U.S. settlers to follow the trails he had explored to Oregon and California. There is some truth to Jessie Benton Frémont's heartfelt tribute to her husband late in life: "All your campfires have become cities."

7

Natural History, Art, and Science

NINETEENTH-CENTURY AMERICANS ENJOYED READING ACCOUNTS of Western exploration by or about such explorers as Meriwether Lewis and William Clark, Zebulon Pike, and John C. Frémont. But they were not satisfied by the written word alone. They wished to see the West with their own eyes. However, most Americans in the nineteenth century lived east of the Mississippi River, and few Americans would ever travel west. Instead, they flocked to museums and exhibitions and other venues in the East. There they could see geological samples, stuffed animals, dried plants, and Native American artifacts brought back by explorers and scientists. Or they went to artists' exhibits to see paintings, prints, and photographs of the Western landscape, animals, and people.

NATURAL HISTORY COLLECTIONS

In the eighteenth century, many people kept cabinets of curiosities in their houses. These collections might include fossils, minerals, seashells, and other natural objects. They might also include Native American artifacts. Artist Charles Willson Peale was a wealthy portrait artist who lived in Philadelphia. He put together a gigantic collection of curiosities and made them available for public viewing. The popularity of Peale's museum increased every year. In 1802, he moved his collection to Philadelphia's Independence Hall.

The exhibits he presented in his museum appealed to and helped shape the popular tastes of the emerging nation. He was a master showman, always looking for new and exciting exhibits to bring to the public.

In the late eighteenth and early nineteenth century, Americans were fascinated with news of the discovery of the fossil remains of ancient and extinct creatures, such as the giant sloth and the mastodon. President Thomas Jefferson was among those interested in fossils, though he was not convinced that the animals they represented had all died out. In 1801, when the fossil bones of a mastodon were accidentally discovered in Newburgh, New York, Peale hurried to the site. President Jefferson lent Peale a navy pumping machine to bail out the flooded pit in which the fossilized bones lay. Peale carried the fossils back to Philadelphia, where the mastodon attracted large crowds to his museum. Peale was always thinking of new ways to attract public attention; among his innovations, he pioneered the use of habitat arrangements for animal specimens so that they appeared to be standing in their natural settings. Such arrangements have remained a standard feature of natural history museum exhibits ever since.

Peale lived until 1827. Peale's museum was poorly managed and it closed in 1846. Many of the exhibits were lost, including the many objects gathered by Lewis and Clark. It was clear that the nation needed a permanent storehouse for its natural, artistic, and historical treasures. In 1846, construction began in Washington, D.C., on a towering brick castle on land near the National Mall. It would soon hold a museum, art gallery, library, and lecture halls. Funding for the building came from a wealthy scientist named James Smithson, who specified that his gift be used for the purpose of establishing a national institution for the "increase and diffusion of knowledge." The new brick building would become known as the Smithsonian Institution. The original building still stands on the Mall today, used as an administrative center for the Smithsonian. Newer buildings now house the institution's ever-expanding artistic, historic, scientific, and natural history collections.

ARTISTS AND NATIVE AMERICANS

Native Americans held a special fascination for some of the best-known U.S. artists of the nineteenth century. Starting in the early 1820s, Charles Bird King painted hundreds of pictures of Native Americans for the federal Bureau of Indian Affairs. These were reproduced in the three-volume *History of the Indian Tribes of North America*, published between 1837 and 1844. King was fascinated by his subjects and idealized them. His chiefs bore a striking resemblance to the classical depictions of ancient noble Romans. But King's portraits were all of Native Americans on the white man's territory, usually of visiting delegations of Native American chiefs who came to Washington, D.C., to meet with the "Great White Father" (a title that indigenous peoples were encouraged to use when referring to the president of the United States). Little could be learned from them about their way of life on their own ground.

George Catlin was one of the first U.S. artists to show the Plains Indians on their own territory. Catlin made a living as a portrait artist. In 1830, he traveled west in search of new subjects. His first stop was St. Louis, where he met William Clark. At the time, Clark was serving as superintendent of Indian Affairs for the Missouri Territory. Peale painted Clark's portrait, a painting that hangs today in the Smithsonian's National Portrait Gallery.

George Catlin made it a personal mission to create accurate depictions of Native Americans on their own territory. He stayed with his Native American subjects and made some of the most memorable paintings done based on his life among the tribes. Here, men of the Choctaw tribe play the traditional ball game with rackets and tall goalposts. Hundreds of players can take part in a game, and other members lay bets on the outcome.

In 1831, Catlin traveled up the Platte River with a detachment of U.S. cavalry. The following year, he took a steamboat up the Missouri. Some of Catlin's most memorable paintings of Native Americans were done in the Mandan and Hidatsa villages in present-day North Dakota. These settlements were made famous by Lewis and Clark's journals. Catlin depicted the daily life of the Mandan as well as their burial and religious rituals. He found much to admire in what he saw. He believed that Native Americans lived a life that white men should envy, "free from . . . a thousand cares and jealousies, which arise from mercenary motives in the civilized world."

Catlin created more than 500 paintings and thousands of sketches during the next four years. He drew his subjects from among 50 tribes he met. These included the Mandan, Blackfoot, Crow, Pawnee, Comanche, Kiowa, and Lakota Indians. Much that Catlin saw on his ventures west sickened him, particularly the wholesale slaughter of the buffalo. As early as 1833, Catlin called for the creation of a great national park to provide a refuge for the buffalo and for the Native Americans who hunted them: "A *nation's Park*, containing man and beast, in all the wild and freshness of their nature's beauty!" he wrote. It was an idea that would take another 40 years to find support in official circles. Yellowstone National Park was created in 1872. By this time, the buffalo was nearly extinct.

Catlin was determined to create a visual record of Plains Indian life. He assembled his paintings and took them on tours in the eastern United States and in Europe. He tried to sell the collection to the U.S. government, but a penny-pinching Congress turned down the deal. After his death, Catlin's gallery was donated to the Smithsonian.

Karl Bodmer's name is often linked to Catlin as a chronicler of Native American life on the upper Missouri and Plains. In 1833, Bodmer was invited by the German prince Maximilian of Wied-Neuwied to join a scientific expedition to the western United States. Maximilian wanted an artist to make a record of the people and the landscape he encountered on his journey. Maximilian's party traveled up the Missouri via steamship and then by keelboat as far as Fort McKenzie, in Blackfoot country in Montana. Then they returned to spend the winter of 1833–1834 in the Mandan and Hidatsa villages.

While his aristocratic sponsor collected specimens and took field notes, Bodmer produced hundreds of watercolor paintings and pencil

JOHN JAMES AUDUBON: THE ARTIST AS PREDATOR

Art and natural history were also closely entwined in the work of John James Audubon. Audubon was born in Haiti in 1785 and raised in France. He moved to the United States in 1803, settling in Kentucky. Audubon had been fascinated by birds since his boyhood and taught himself to paint so that he could portray their appearance in the wild. He also taught himself to hunt, because in order to paint birds accurately, he needed specimens to study. He became expert at wiring his newly killed specimens into lifelike postures, creating the illusion he was painting his birds from close observation in nature. Audubon traveled widely to collect his specimens, starting with trips on the Mississippi River, then heading westward up the Missouri and the Yellowstone rivers, as well as exploring the Atlantic and Gulf coasts.

In 1824, Audubon went to Philadelphia seeking financial support to publish a collection of his bird paintings. He passed himself off as a kind of artistic mountain man, dressing in buckskins and slicking back his hair with bear grease. He failed to win support from the city's artistic and scientific community, so in 1826 he went to England to try his luck. The buckskins went over better with potential English patrons, and Audubon secured the support he needed for his project.

Between 1826 and 1838 Audubon produced his masterwork. *The Birds of America* featured life-size colored portraits of more than 1,000 species. The five-volume *Ornithological Biography* followed, with detailed essays on each of the birds depicted in his prints. Audubon's name became permanently linked to bird-watching and appreciation. His paintings proved so popular because, in addition to their accuracy, they also told stories about individual birds— about their mating habits, their sociability, and, most dramatically, about their lives and deaths. Many of his best bird paintings show predatory birds at the moment they were capturing their prey, such as his golden eagle with a white rabbit in its claws. Audubon seemed to identify with his birds. He was, after all, a kind of predator himself, who killed in order to portray the living beauty of his prey.

sketches. They included notable portraits of Native American chiefs, as well as striking landscapes of the sandstone formations that line the upper Missouri River. The party returned to Europe in July 1834. Back home, Prince Maximilian published an account of his expedition titled *Travels in the Interior of North America*, illustrated by 81 engravings from Bodmer's paintings and sketches. Bodmer never returned to the United States, but most of his paintings of Native Americans wound up in the Joslyn Art Museum in Omaha, Nebraska.

LANDSCAPE ARTISTS

While Catlin, Bodmer, and others were fascinated by western Native Americans, other artists concentrated on depicting the western landscape in all its natural glory. Albert Bierstadt became one of the most famous western artists of the generation following Catlin and Bodmer. Bierstadt decided to go west in 1858. With a government expedition, he crossed the South Pass in the Rockies. He then headed on his own into the Wind River region. He was amazed by the beauty of the western mountains. He found the western mountains far superior to those of the northeastern United States. The Rockies' "jagged summits," he wrote:

> [C]overed with snow and mingling with clouds, present a scene which every lover of landscape would gaze upon in unqualified delight. . . . We see many spots in the scenery that remind us of our New Hampshire and Catskill hills, but when we look up and measure the mighty perpendicular cliffs that rise hundreds of feet aloft, all capped with snow, we then realize that we are among a different class of mountains.

Returning to New York, he turned his sketches of the Rockies into grand paintings of western scenes. He returned west in 1863 and sketched Yosemite Valley. In 1880, he visited and sketched the Yellowstone area. Bierstadt's paintings were often inaccurate but still immensely popular. One of them sold for $15,000, about $1.5 million today.

The landscape artist Thomas Moran was another western painter who became famous and wealthy. Moran headed to Yellowstone in 1871. He sketched the Gardiner River, Mammoth Hot Springs, Liberty Cap, and Tower Fall, among other sites. Moran's paintings of the

Yellowstone region created a sensation when they were displayed in the East. One was 7-by-12-foot (2-by-3-m) *The Grand Canyon of the Yellowstone*, was purchased by the U.S. government for $10,000 for display in the U.S. Capitol. Two years later, Congress purchased Moran's *The Chasm of the Colorado.* This painting showed the Grand Canyon, a site Moran found deeply stirring: "The whole gorge for miles lay beneath us and it was by far the most awfully grand and impressive scene that I have ever yet seen," he wrote home to his wife. "A sort of suppressed sort of roar comes up constantly from the chasm but with that exception everything impresses you with awful stillness." Moran believed that America's natural beauty should fill its citizens with the love of their own nation. "That there is a nationalism in art needs no proof," he would write. "It is bred from a knowledge of and sympathy with [one's own] surroundings and no foreigner can imbue himself with a spirit of a country not his own. Therefore he should paint his own land. . . ."

WESTERN PHOTOGRAPHY

In the 1850s, a new technique was perfected. Cameras recorded images on glass negatives, from which many copies could be made. Thus was born the modern art of photography. One of the first western explorers to use photography was Lieutenant Joseph C. Ives of the Army Corps of Topographical Engineers. Ives took a camera and portable darkroom equipment with him on his 1857 expedition to the Grand Canyon. Only one of the photographs he took, near the mouth of the Colorado, survives.

Henry Youle Hind's 1858 Red River expedition enjoyed more success with the new technology. Toronto photographer Humphrey Lloyd Hime traveled with the Hind Expedition. His photographs of the Canadian prairie were reproduced in the official expedition report. They were also displayed in galleries, with prints sold to the general public.

After the Civil War, many photographers headed west. They joined the survey parties that finalized the route for the transcontinental railroad. One of the most famous photographic images of this time is Andrew J. Russell's "East Meets West at the Laying of the Last Rail." This photograph shows the moment when the tracks of the Union Pacific and Central Pacific railroads were linked on May 10, 1869, at Promontory Point, Utah.

On May 10, 1869, the Union Pacific and Central Pacific railroads met near Promontory Point, Utah, at Promontory Summit to drive the final spike connecting the two railroads. This photograph is one of the most famous images of the postwar era.

THE ART OF WILD WEST NOSTALGIA

In the later decades of the nineteenth century, the great era of western exploration came to an end. A new western hero was taking the place in popular imagination that had earlier been held by explorers. Now it was the turn of the cowboy to be celebrated, in pulp fiction and touring "Wild West" shows. They were seen as examples of manly courage and rugged individualism on the frontier, loners bound by a code of honor riding through a dangerous land. The era of the cowboys lasted only about 20 years; afterward, the barbed-wire fencing of the open range and the expansion of the railroads made the trail drive unnecessary. But in those 20 years they provided an enduring set of images that for years to come helped define not only the western experience but the American character.

Although as many as one in four cowboys was African American, another one in four was Mexican American, and there were Native American cowboys as well, none of them seemed to make much impression on the popular imagination. The cowboy who lived on in the nation's mythology was a white man whose skill with a six-gun gave him the power necessary to tame a savage land and its dark-skinned inhabitants. This image of the cowboy was, in its early days, largely the creation of the artist Frederic Remington, who despised Native Americans and other nonwhites.

Remington, born in Canton, New York, in 1861, came west as a journalist in the 1880s, in the glory days of the cattle drives. As a reporter for *Harper's Weekly* and other eastern magazines, he covered the U.S. Army's campaigns against the Apache and Lakota. He provided illustrations as well for his stories. Remington's works were extremely popular. Sales of his paintings and his bronzes, including his 1895 sculpture the *Bronco Buster,* made him a wealthy man. Remington's imagery and prejudices would have a lasting influence, in the form of countless cowboy-and-Indian movies turned out by Hollywood in the first half of the twentieth century.

THE MAKING OF A GEOLOGIST

John Wesley "Wes" Powell was born in the village of Mount Morris in western New York on March 24, 1834. His father, Joseph, was a restless man, always on the lookout for a better opportunity for himself and his family. In 1838, when Wes was four years old, he and his family moved west to a new home in Jackson County, Ohio.

His father's fervent opposition to slavery would have a large impact on his life. Joseph Powell's abolitionism made him unpopular with many of his neighbors and led to his son being bullied in the local public school. Young Wes was sent instead to study with George Crookham, a friend of the Powells. Crookham, an abolitionist whose farm was a stop on the Underground Railroad, was an amateur naturalist who had his own little museum. It was filled with plant, animal, and fossil specimens, as well as Native American artifacts. Thanks to Crookham, Powell became a convert to the study of nature.

When the hostility of their Ohio neighbors grew too much to endure, the Powells moved again, in 1846, to Wisconsin. At 12 years old, Powell gave up his education to take on a grown-up's share of the work in running the family farm. He left home at age 16 for a year of schooling at a local school in Janesville, Wisconsin.

By age 18, Powell was teaching in a one-room schoolhouse in Wisconsin. He taught himself while instructing his students. He enrolled at Illinois College in Jacksonville, Illinois. There, he studied the sciences, Greek, and Latin, as well as practical subjects like surveying. In 1857, he transferred to the Illinois Institute at Wheaton. The following spring, he transferred again, to Oberlin College in Ohio. He eventually left college without a degree. Nonetheless, by the standards of nineteenth-century America, his three years of college instruction placed him among the ranks of the highly educated. He took a job teaching school in Hennepin, Illinois, in 1859. Within a year, at age 26, he was the school principal.

Powell loved to be outdoors. He took trips along the riverways of the Midwest. He rowed along the Mississippi, the Ohio, and the Illinois rivers, rambling as far north as Wisconsin and as far south as New Orleans. He gathered shells of freshwater mollusks on his journeys. In 1858, he became a curator at the Illinois State Natural History Society. He was elected secretary of the Illinois State Natural History Society in March 1861.

When the Civil War began, Powell responded to President Abraham Lincoln's call for volunteers to defend the Union. He was promoted to lieutenant and then captain. On April 6, 1862, Powell and his men were attacked by Confederate soldiers. Powell was struck in the right wrist by a bullet. Two days later an army surgeon amputated his right arm just below the elbow. Powell was lucky. He had lost an arm, but he would live. Powell returned to his unit. He was promoted to major and retired from the army in January 1865. For the rest of his life, he would be called "Major Powell."

POWELL EXPLORES THE WEST

After working as a professor of science at Illinois State Normal University, Powell decided to make his mark as an explorer. He hoped to fill in the blank spaces on the western map of the United States. In 1867 he set off westward across the plains. His party of 12 included friends, students, his wife, his brother, and his brother-in-law. They were all new to the West and an unlikely team of explorers. However, the trail they followed to the Colorado Rockies had become a well-traveled route.

Two days after Independence Day, Powell's party arrived in Denver. They headed into the Rockies on a southerly route. On July 27–28, they climbed Pike's Peak. They went down to South Park, where they spent several weeks gathering animal, plant, and mineral specimens. The specimens they gathered would look good on the shelves of Illinois museums.

By September most of the party had left for points east. Powell and his wife remained in Colorado, heading up to Middle Park in the Rockies. There they met Jack Sumner, who ran a trading post in Hot Sulphur Springs. With Sumner, Powell began to consider the idea of a real trip into the unknown. He dreamed of taking the trip by boat down the Green River to the Colorado all the way to its mouth on the Gulf of California. That expedition would have to wait until Powell raised more money and recruited more explorers. But he did visit the headwaters of what was then known as the Grand River, later renamed the upper Colorado River, his first glimpse of the waters that would make him famous.

Powell returned to Colorado in 1868. He and his group built cabins along the White River, near present-day Meeker, Colorado. During the winter, Powell traveled south. He explored the Grand River and the White and Green rivers, planning his trip down the Colorado. He gathered specimens. He also studied the language and customs of the Ute. In spring 1869, he headed home to Illinois to order boats built in Chicago.

Powell returned in May with his new boats and more explorers. They successfully sailed down the Colorado. The news of the expedition's success was telegraphed to the eastern newspapers in September 1869. Powell became a national hero. His triumph seemed all the greater because rumors had surfaced earlier that summer that he and all his party had been swept away by the river's rapids and would never be seen again.

Powell offered stirring lectures about the trip. He later wrote about it in magazine articles and books. The boat ride down the Colorado had been a great adventurous feat. Yet, it yielded few scientific results. Powell had been forced to abandon many of the specimens he had gathered. Powell hoped to return and spend more time studying the great river.

On July 12, 1870, Congress approved giving Powell $10,000 to survey the Colorado region. This was the first support he had gained from the federal government. In the late summer and early fall of 1870, Powell returned to Colorado. He scouted along the northern rim of the Grand Canyon. He chose places to leave supplies for the following year's expedition and made friendly contact with local Native Americans.

On May 22, 1871, Powell set off once again toward the Colorado. This time his expedition consisted of 11 members traveling in three boats. Powell's brother-in-law, Almon Harris Thompson, was one of three topographers on the 1871 expedition. Thompson served as Powell's second-in-command. The 17-year-old artist Frederick Samuel Dellenbaugh joined them, as did photographer E.O. Beaman.

The expedition proceeded downriver. The boats traveled slower than they had in 1869. It took four and a half months to travel from Green River Station to the foot of Glen Canyon. The 1869 expedition had covered this distance in just two months. In the Lodore Canyon they passed the wreck of the *No-Name*. This was the boat Powell had lost in the rapids in 1869. This time they sailed through the canyon without incident.

While Powell explored neighboring canyonlands on horseback that summer and made side trips to Salt Lake City, Thompson took command on the water. Powell met up again with his men in the boats at the end of August. He sailed downriver as far as the Crossing of the Fathers, then set off again overland. His men made further progress to the mouth of the Paria River. They left the boats there for the winter and headed to their winter camp at Kanab. Powell and some of the party surveyed the land north of the Grand Canyon in southern Utah and Arizona before Powell headed off to Washington in early 1872. He planned to lobby for additional funding for his survey. Powell rejoined the men on the river the following August. They sailed deep into the Grand Canyon. The unusually high waters and leaky boats soon forced them to abandon the river.

The 1871–1872 expedition was not as dramatic as Powell's first trip down the Colorado in 1869. However, its scientific achievements

During his travels, John Wesley Powell developed friendly relations with the Native Americans. Here he is pictured with Paiute chief Tau-gu.

were greater. The team discovered the last unknown river in the United States, the Escalante. Almon Thompson completed a topographic map of the region in February 1873. This was the first detailed mapping of the Green and Colorado rivers. The expedition's photographs included the first photographs ever taken from the canyon's floor.

In 1879, Congress brought all federal surveying efforts under a single administrative roof. It created the U.S. Geological Survey (USGS). This government agency is part of the Department of the Interior. In 1881, Powell became its director. He attracted some of the country's most talented geologists and geographers to work for the USGS. The men, who became known as "Powell's Boys," did the fieldwork while Powell focused on lobbying and public relations.

A LIFE'S WORK COMPLETED

Powell's ideas on land-use regulation won him powerful enemies among western congressmen and their wealthy constituents, including mine owners and big ranchers. In the 1890s, Congress began cutting the USGS budget. This was a clear signal that Powell had fallen into official disfavor. In 1894, in poor health, he stepped down as USGS director. He continued to carry out official duties as director of the Bureau of Ethnology for the rest of his life.

Powell died at his summer home in Haven, Maine, on September 23, 1902. Major Powell was buried with full military honors in Arlington National Cemetery. In his lifetime he made 30 trips exploring the western United States. At the time of his death, he and his companions from 1869 remained the only people known to have traveled the length of the Colorado River from Green River Station to the mouth of the Grand Canyon. They are among the great scientist and artist explorers of the American West.

8

The Exploration
of Alaska

ALASKA IS THE LARGEST STATE IN THE UNITED STATES. ITS territory contains nearly 600,000 square miles (965,606 sq km). This one state is equal in size to about one-fifth of the rest of the United States. It has more than 6,600 miles (10,621 km) of coastline. This is more than the combined length of the eastern and western seaboards of the lower United States. Alaska is bounded on the north by the Arctic Ocean, to the west by the Bering Sea, and to the south by the Pacific Ocean. It contains more than 20,000 miles (32,186 km) of inland waters, more than any other state. It is home to the United States's highest mountain, 20,320-foot (932,701-km) Mount Denali (formerly Mount McKinley), and the next 15 highest summits.

A third of Alaska lies above the Arctic Circle. Most of the rest of the state is subarctic in climate. Temperatures can drop as low as 70 degrees below zero in the winters. In warmer seasons, there are huge swarms of ferocious mosquitoes. All in all, Alaska has offered many challenges to those who would explore it. It earned the designation of North America's "last frontier."

EARLY ALASKAN EXPLORATION
AND SETTLEMENT

North America's last frontier was in fact the first to know human visitors. Some 15,000 to 18,000 years ago, Native Peoples crossed a land bridge from Asia to Alaska. About 11,000 years ago the last ice age ended. Melting glacier waters raised the level of the sea enough to cover this land bridge. Land migration ended. Other people from Siberia probably arrived by small boats, perhaps 8,000 years ago.

At the beginning of the eighteenth century, about 50,000 people lived in Alaska. The Inuit lived on the coast of the Alaska mainland and some of the coastal islands. The Aleut lived on the Alaskan Peninsula and the rugged Aleutians. The Aleutians are a chain of islands that stretch westward 1,200 miles (1,931 km) toward Siberia. Native Americans lived in the northeast and interior regions. These Alaskan peoples spoke different languages. They worshiped different gods. Depending on habitat, some lived primarily on salmon. Others hunted and ate caribou. Still others lived on whale, seal, or sea lion meat.

THE ORIGINS OF RUSSIAN AMERICA

At the end of the sixteenth century, Russian settlers were moving eastward across Siberia. The Cossacks served the Russian czars as warriors and led frontier exploration. By the 1630s, Cossack fur hunters had built an outpost on the Pacific Ocean at Okhotsk. From the native Yupik people the Cossacks heard rumors of a "great land" lying even farther to the east. The Yupik word for it sounded to the Russians like "A-la-a-ska."

In 1725, Czar Peter the Great of Russia ordered a 44-year-old Danish-born sailor named Vitus Bering to explore the seas off the coast of Siberia. Three years later, Bering sailed into the waters separating Siberia's Chukotsk Peninsula from Alaska's Seward Peninsula. Later, in honor of Bering, this would be named the Bering Strait. Bering turned back before seeing the great land rumored to lie farther to the east.

In 1732, Russian navigator Ivan Fedorov and surveyor Mikhail Gvozdev reached the Alaskan coast. Fedorov and Gvozdev called the new land *bolshaya zemlaya*, or "big land." But they did not realize that they had reached America.

In 1741, Bering and Alexei Chirikov set out on the Great Northern or Second Kamchatka Expedition. They sailed in two boats, the *St. Peter*, under Bering's command, and the *St. Paul*, under Chirikov's. Their ships were separated by a storm. Both independently came within sight of the Alaskan mainland. Unlike Fedorov and Gvozdev, Bering and Chirikov knew that the land they had arrived at was part of the North American continent. Chirikov spied present-day Prince of Wales Island on July 15, 1741, but, having lost his longboats, he failed to land. Bering sighted

Inuit have traditionally lived in areas stretching from Alaska across northern Canada to Greenland. Today, they still hunt whales, walruses, caribou, seal, polar bears, and birds. In this 1930s photograph, two Inuit children hold the tusks of a large walrus, which was probably killed for food.

18,008-foot- (28,981-km-) high Mount St. Elias on July 16. He landed a few days later on Cape St. Elias, on the Gulf of Alaska.

Bering would never see Russia again. Short of provisions and desperate to make landfall on their return voyage, on November 5 he and his crew put in at an island now known as Bering Island. They were still 200 miles (321 km) from their home port. There, Bering's beached ship was washed offshore and wrecked by the pounding of winter waves. Bering died of scurvy that December. About half his crew survived to return home in a small boat. But they brought back something of great value—furs from the sea otters that lived on Bering Island.

The furs Bering's crew brought to Siberia spurred further Russian exploration. Between the mid-1740s and the mid-1760s, Russian fur traders worked their way steadily eastward. They moved from island to island through the Aleutians until they reached the Alaskan mainland. Fur trader Grigorii Shelikhov built the first permanent Russian outpost in North America in 1784. It lay on the southwestern coast of Kodiak Island. Soon, seven rival Russian fur companies competed in the region. In 1799, Russian czar Paul I issued an imperial charter creating a trade monopoly in Alaska. The company was modeled on the Hudson's Bay Company and known as the Russian-American Company.

Like the Hudson's Bay Company, the Russian-American Company was both a commercial enterprise and an agent of colonial power. The company's manager, Aleksandr Baranov, ruled Russian America with an iron hand, bloodily putting down native rebellions. But there were never more than a few hundred Russians administering this trading empire, from a chain of outposts running from Sitka to Kodiak. They might not have stood up to a serious military challenge from Spain or England. Both of these countries had sent their own explorers to the region in the eighteenth century. Fortunately for the Russians, their chief European rivals in the region were drawn into a prolonged conflict with Napoleonic France at the start of the nineteenth century.

The Russians dreamed of extending their own empire southward. In 1812, Russian traders built Fort Ross, 90 miles (144 km) north of San Francisco. But there were fewer and fewer furs. Pressure from Spanish authorities forced the Russians out of Fort Ross. In 1841, they sold the outpost to California settler John Sutter.

Back in Alaska, the Russians made little progress exploring. In the 1830s and 1840s, Russian explorers mapped some rivers inland. However, they followed none of them to their headwaters. They also did not attempt to explore the surrounding lands. Russian explorers in the 1830s spotted a high, distant peak and noted it on their maps. But the Russians were more interested in the coast than the interior. The mountain disappeared from their later maps of Alaska. It was later known as McKinley and then, today, as Denali.

The Russians had found gold, coal, and oil deposits. They continued to take valuable furs from the region. Still, Russia's rulers began to view Alaska as more trouble than it was worth. Russia went to war with Britain and France in the Crimea in 1853. The Russians feared that the British might strike at their North American empire. If the Russians had to face another power from across the Bering Strait, they would rather have it be the Americans than the British.

SEWARD'S FOLLY

Russian-American relations were friendly in these years. Many Russian furs found their way to China aboard U.S. merchant ships. In 1824, the U.S. and Russian governments signed a treaty. The Russians gave up land claims in North America below 54°40' latitude (54 degrees, 40 minutes). Americans showed little interest in Alaska at this time. The territory fell into U.S. hands more as a result of Russian rather than U.S. initiative.

In 1867, the United States bought Alaska from Russia for $7.2 million. This price worked out to about 2 cents an acre. Many Americans at the time thought it a waste of good money. They called this latest addition to U.S. territory "The New National Refrigerator." But U.S. Secretary of State William H. Seward knew what he was doing when he negotiated the deal. Alaska, he declared, would prove a "great fishery, forest and mineral storehouse." Its possession cemented U.S. strategic power in the North Pacific. It provided an advance base for military and commercial expansion in Asia. It also stopped British ambitions in the region.

AMERICAN EXPLORATION BEGINS

Even before Alaska was officially a U.S. territory, U.S. explorers were at work. Among the first was Robert Kennicott. He was born in New Orleans in 1835 and raised in Illinois. He became curator of the Northwestern University Museum of Natural History. In 1860–1861, Kennicott led an expedition sponsored by the Chicago Academy of Sciences and the Smithsonian Institution. Kennicott's party traveled through northwest Canada and deep into the interior of Alaska. He sent back 40 crates of specimens and Native American artifacts. Kennicott became an expert on the natural history of the Canadian Northwest.

In 1865, Kennicott returned to the region. This time he worked for the Western Union Telegraph Company. The first transcontinental telegraph line had only recently been built. It allowed instantaneous communication between the East and West coasts. Western Union hoped to extend its communication link to Europe. Attempts to lay down a

In 1867, the Russian government signed over Alaska to the United States for $7.2 million. Americans thought it was a foolish purchase, calling it Seward's Folly after William H. Seward, who negotiated the deal. Pictured, Russian and American diplomats sign the Alaska Purchase Treaty.

transatlantic cable had failed. Western Union hoped to run its telegraph lines across the Bering Strait and Siberia to connect with European lines. It was a bold plan. The company turned to Kennicott for help.

Kennicott led the Russian-American Telegraph Expedition. His team included a "scientific corps." These scientists studied Alaska's climate, plants, and animals. They sent home many valuable specimens to the Smithsonian Institution. Later, they wrote papers on Alaskan climate, geology, zoology, and botany. But the expedition was poorly organized and led. It was made irrelevant when an Atlantic telegraph cable was finally laid in 1867. To make matters worse, Kennicott died along the Yukon River on May 13, 1866. He had a heart attack while taking compass bearings.

William Healey Dall took over the expedition. Dall became the most important figure in Alaskan exploration for the rest of the nineteenth century. He wrote a vivid account of his first look at the Yukon River in his book *Alaska and Its Resources*:

[T]here lay a stretch of forty miles of this great, broad, snow-covered river, with broken fragments of ice-cakes glowing in the ruddy light of the setting sun; the low opposite shore, three miles away, seemed a mere black streak on the horizon. A few islands covered with dark evergreens were in sight above. Below, a faint purple tinged the snowy crests of far-off mountains, whose height, though not extreme, seemed greater from the low banks near me and the clear sky beyond. This was the river I had read and dreamed of, which had seemed as if shrouded in mystery, in spite of the tales of those who had seen it. On its banks live thousands who know neither its outlet nor its source, who look to it for food and even for clothing, and, recognizing its magnificence, call themselves proudly men of the Yukon.

Alaska was now U.S. territory. Dall found new sponsors for his research among U.S. government agencies. He spent several years mapping the Alaskan coastline for the U.S. Coast Survey. He explored mountains and glaciers. He studied the Aleut and the Inuit people. He sent many specimens back to U.S. museums, including large collections of mollusks. And he published extensively. Dall wrote 400 scientific papers about his discoveries.

MILITARY EXPLORERS

In its first years as a U.S. territory, Alaska was governed by the military. U.S. Army explorers extended knowledge of the Alaskan interior. In 1869, army captain Charles Raymond took a steamboat up the Yukon. He reached the Hudson's Bay Company trading post at Fort Yukon. The trading post had been founded in 1847. The Russians had shown little interest in its existence. Now the Americans wanted to know if it lay in Canadian or U.S. territory. The Yukon bisects Alaska. It had been explored before. But Raymond was the first to do so by steamboat. His journey resulted in a more accurate map of the upper Yukon. Fort Yukon, it turned out, was in U.S. territory. Captain Raymond ordered the Hudson's Bay Company men to pack up and head home.

The army knew the Yukon River was important. In 1883, Lieutenant Frederick Schwatka sailed from its headwaters to its mouth on the Bering Sea. Military explorers also began to map other Alaskan rivers.

The most accomplished explorer was army lieutenant Henry Tureman Allen. Allen welcomed his assignment to Alaska in 1884. "I am willing to forgo almost any benefit that I might receive by going east," Allen wrote his fiancée the previous year, "for an attempt at exploration in Alaska." He got his wish in 1885. Allen explored the Copper, Tanana, and Koyukuk rivers. He traveled about 1,500 miles (2,414 km) through unexplored wilderness in just five months. General Nelson A. Miles was commander of the U.S. Army's Northwest Department at the time. He said that Allen's achievement "exceeded all explorations on the American continent since Lewis and Clark. . . ."

CIVILIAN EXPLORERS, SCIENTISTS, AND TOURISTS

Toward the end of the century, the U.S. Geological Survey started mapping the Alaskan interior. Geologist Alfred Hulse Brooks became the best known of the USGS men in Alaska. He was appointed head of the Alaska section of the Geological Survey in 1903. Alaska's Brooks Range was named for him. It contains the highest mountains lying above the Arctic Circle.

Many other explorers helped fill in the Alaskan map. Naturalist and travel writer John Muir made the first of many trips to Alaska in 1879. Muir discovered Glacier Bay. It soon became an Alaskan tourist attraction. Muir found in Alaska the unspoiled wilderness that was becoming increasingly hard to find in the lower United States. He wrote beautiful descriptions of his discoveries. His 1888 account tells of a steamer trip up the Stikeen River. The river, he noted, flowed first in a westerly direction:

> [T]hrough grassy, undulating plains, darkened here and there with passages of forest; then, curving southward and receiving numerous tributaries from the north, it enters the Coast Range and sweeps across it to the sea through a canyon that is sculptured like Yosemite, and is more than a hundred miles long, one to three miles wide at the bottom, and from five to eight thousand feet deep, marvelously beautiful and inspiring from end to end. . . . Back of the walls, and thousands of feet above them, innumerable peaks and spires and domes of ice and snow tower grandly

into the deep blue sky. . . . Wondrous, too are the changes depen-
dent on the weather—avalanches from the heights, booming and
resounding from cliff to cliff, and storm-winds from the arctic high-
lands sweeping the canyon like a flood, filling the air with ice-dust,
and robing rock, glacier and forest in spotless white.

Tourists were few and far between in the early days of Alaskan settlement. Generally, those who came to Alaska in the nineteenth century
as visitors were used to a rugged outdoor life. A group of mountaineers
were lured by the high summits. The mountains were higher than those
found in the lower United States or the European Alps. In 1886, the *New
York Times* sponsored a mountaineering expedition to Mount St. Elias.
This was the same 18,000-foot (5,486-m)-high mountain that Bering
had spotted back in 1741. They failed. A U.S. Geological Survey party in
the early 1890s had no better luck. Italian climbers finally reached the
summit in 1897. They were led by Prince Luigi Amadeo di Savoia, the
duke of Abruzzi.

The most famous private expedition to Alaska was that of Edward
Henry Harriman in 1899. Harriman was one of the wealthiest men in
America. His fortune at century's end was estimated at $60 million.
Told by his doctor to take a long vacation for his health, he chose a
rather unusual one. He chartered a luxurious passenger ship and set
sail for Alaska. More than 100 passengers and crew joined him. They
explored the northwestern coast. For Harriman it was primarily a hunting trip. He shot a huge Kodiak bear on Kodiak Island. He was disap-
pointed, as he had wanted to kill a polar bear.

Harriman was joined by scientists, artists, and writers. These
included William Henry Dall and John Muir. Harriman's scientists
gathered thousands of plant, animal, and mineral specimens. They also
collected Inuit, Aleut, and Native American artifacts. They mapped glaciers. They discovered a new fjord. After the expedition was over, Harriman sponsored the writing and publication of a 13-volume report on
their findings. It was called *The Harriman Alaska Series.*

The explorers could return to the comforts of Harriman's passenger
ship at the end of a long day's hike. They enjoyed a level of luxury that
previous generations of explorers would never have dreamed possible.
As John Muir noted in a letter to Harriman's children after the trip:

JACK LONDON AND THE ROMANCE OF ALASKA

Jack London's novel *The Call of the Wild* is one of the most famous dog stories ever written. In the book, a pampered house pet named Buck learns to survive in the Alaskan wilderness during the time of the gold rush. The book made London a wealthy man. It was a welcome change for Jack London, who was born into poverty in San Francisco in 1876. For many years he supported himself by hard work for low wages. Then, in 1897, he headed off to Alaska to try his luck as a gold prospector.

London did not find many golden nuggets in Alaska, but he did find a golden literary subject to write about: wilderness survival. In 1898, at age 22, he sold his first short story, "To the Man on the Trail." This tale drew on his experiences in Alaska. *The Call of the Wild* followed in 1903. *The Call of the Wild* contributed to the romance of Alaska as the "last frontier." Alaska was a place where men could test themselves against the elements and go back to a time before more civilized settings. "There is an ecstasy that marks the summit of life, and beyond which life cannot rise," London wrote near the end of his novel. "And such is the paradox of living, this ecstasy comes when one is most alive, and it comes as a complete forgetfulness that one is alive. . . . [I]t came to Buck leading the pack, sounding the old wolf-cry, straining after the food that was alive and that fled swiftly before him during the moonlight."

"On the *Elder* I found not only the fields I liked best to study, but a hotel, a club, and a home together with a floating university. I enjoyed the instruction and companionship of a lot of the best fellows imaginable." The Harriman Expedition helped transform the popular view in the United States that Alaska was a barren wasteland. The expedition sowed the seeds for the growth of the Alaskan tourist industry.

THE LAST DAYS OF THE LAST FRONTIER

The first Americans to come to Alaska came for furs. Then they came for salmon. But growth among the non-Native population was slow. There were fewer Alaskans of European descent in 1870 than in 1840. According to the 1880 census, there were only 430 white Alaskans, compared to about 33,000 Alaska Natives.

Ten years later, in 1890, there were about 4,300 whites. By the turn of the century, there were more than 30,000 whites. Gold made the sudden difference. There were modest gold strikes in the 1870s and 1880s. The strikes attracted a few thousand prospectors. A major strike on Bonanza Creek in the Canadian Klondike in 1896 brought tens of thousands to the Canadian Yukon and Alaska.

Alaska continues to draw new settlers. Of the 627,000 Alaskans counted in the 2000 census, more than 250,000 lived in Anchorage or its immediate vicinity. Another 80,000 lived in Fairbanks and neighboring communities. Four out of five Alaskans lived in the lower third of the state. As a recent study by Stephen Haycox, professor of history at the University of Alaska in Anchorage, noted: "Most Alaskans drive ordinary cars on asphalt streets to platted subdivisions of framed houses with unruly grass and unruly children." Even the most remote Native villages in the northern and western Alaskan backcountry are linked by satellite television, telephones, and light air transportation to the larger communities along Alaska's southern coast. The call of the wild may still echo for some, but it echoes ever more faintly.

9

Wilderness Preservation

By the end of the nineteenth century, the era of the American frontier was ending. Thanks to explorers, no blank spaces on the map remained to be filled in. The Native American tribes once owned all the western lands. Now, they were penned up on reservations. Their numbers were dwindling. Their future survival was uncertain. Ranchers were overgrazing lands. Lumber workers were clear-cutting forests. Other practices were ruining millions of acres of former wilderness land. Hunting and the destruction of habitat were killing off native species of animals. There were few buffalo where once millions had ranged across the plains. The numbers of grizzly bears, beavers, gray wolves, caribou, cutthroat trout, bighorn sheep, and prairie dogs were greatly reduced.

Telegraph lines crisscrossed the plains. Railroads linked the coasts. The open range was fenced off with barbed wire. Americans moved west in ever-increasing numbers. By the start of the twentieth century, San Francisco was one of the nation's 10 largest cities. One hundred years later, six of the nation's 10 largest cities lay west of the Mississippi. With each passing year, the wild West was becoming more tame. It was then that Americans began to rediscover the virtues of wilderness.

TEDDY ROOSEVELT

Theodore ("Teddy") Roosevelt Jr. was born in 1858 in New York City. His family was very wealthy, and his father, Theodore Sr., showered his children with privileges. They traveled to Europe. They went to the best schools. He also gave his children a sense of social obligation, donating to many worthy causes. He helped found New York City's American Museum of Natural History.

Teddy was a sickly child. He was underweight and suffered from asthma and poor eyesight. But he was determined to build up his health. He took up boxing and horseback riding. He exercised in the gym his father built in the family mansion.

Young Teddy was also fascinated by nature. At age 10, he wrote a letter complaining about a tree being cut down. He taught himself taxidermy and began a collection of stuffed birds and animals while still a child. He later donated them to the American Museum of Natural History and the Smithsonian Institution. At Harvard University he studied American and natural history. Upon graduation, he entered the rough and tumble world of New York state politics. He won election to the New York State Assembly in 1881, at age 23.

In 1883, Roosevelt made his first trip to the Dakota badlands. He went there, in part, because of his interest in the outdoors. But there may have been other reasons as well. A New York newspaper had called him unmanly and "chief of the dudes." A "dude" in western slang referred to someone coming from the East who had more money than common sense or toughness. Being chief of the dudes was an insult.

Roosevelt wanted to prove that he was not just another "dude." He bought a ranch and a herd of cattle in North Dakota in 1883. He spent whole days on horseback, taking part in cattle roundups and hunting buffalo. He even helped the local sheriff chase cattle thieves. He posed for photographs to suggest the image he wanted to show the voters back east. In one he wore a fringed buckskin costume, looking like a version of an early nineteenth-century mountain man. In another photograph he was dressed as a cowboy.

In 1884, Alice, his wife, died. Saddened by this tragedy, he headed back west to the Dakotas. The long hours in the saddle hardened him. "What a change!" one eastern newspaper wrote on his return. Roosevelt "is now brown as a berry and has increased 30 pounds in weight . . ." His voice was "hearty and strong enough to drive oxen." His career in politics took off. He was the first politician since John C. Frémont to successfully play on the U.S. attachment to frontier ideals. To hear Roosevelt tell it, he was a frontiersman first and a politician only in his

Theodore Roosevelt, twenty-sixth president of the United States, used his office to pass legislation advocating the efficient use of natural resources. Still, Roosevelt enjoyed hunting and at times compromised wilderness preservation in order to bring back new animal specimens for various museums.

spare time. "[T]here are few sensations," he once wrote, that "I prefer to that of galloping over these rolling, limitless prairies, rifle in hand."

Roosevelt was the perfect politician for a nation that was looking abroad to new frontiers. When war with Spain broke out in 1898, Roosevelt raised a group of volunteers. They were called the "Rough Riders." He led them in battle at San Juan Hill in Cuba. He returned to the United States after the Spanish-American War as a national hero. He was elected governor of New York in 1898, then vice president of the United States in 1900. By now he was seen as a rough-riding cowboy who knew how to get things done in Washington, as well as out on the range.

In 1899, he had delivered a speech in Chicago that he called "The Strenuous Life." It would be his most famous speech. In it, he summed up the philosophy by which he lived his own life and hoped his countrymen would also follow it:

> In speaking to you, men of the greatest city of the West, men of the State which gave to the country Lincoln and Grant, men who preeminently and distinctly embody all that is most American in the American character, I wish to preach, not the doctrine of ignoble ease, but the doctrine of the strenuous life, the life of toil and effort, of labor and strife, to preach that highest form of success which comes, not to the man who desires mere easy peace, but to the man who does not shrink from danger, from hardship, or from bitter toil, and who out of these wins the splendid ultimate triumph.

For Roosevelt, the strenuous life was tied to a life lived outdoors. In 1887, Roosevelt cofounded the Boone and Crockett Club. This was a group of wealthy hunters who were interested in conservation. Roosevelt loved to kill big animals like buffalo, but he also knew that the buffalo were dying out. They would disappear entirely unless something was done to protect them.

Roosevelt was hiking on Mount Marcy, the highest summit in New York's Adirondack Mountains, when he learned of the death of President William McKinley, killed by an assassin's bullet. Roosevelt became president. He could now help other Americans pursue the "strenuous life." One of the ways he would do so was by saving America's remaining wilderness areas.

JOHN MUIR

John Muir was another adopted son of the West. Born in Scotland in 1838, Muir moved with his family to Wisconsin in 1849. At age 30, he moved on by himself to California. Even more than Roosevelt, Muir was drawn to the wilderness. He moved to a cabin in Yosemite Valley and supported himself with a variety of jobs, from sheepherder to sawmill operator. In every spare moment, he explored the Sierra Nevada. Recalling his first view of the mountain range, he would later write, "It seemed to me the Sierra should be called . . . the Range of Light . . . the most divinely beautiful of all the mountain chains I have ever seen."

Muir became an expert on the geology, geography, and ecology of the Sierra Nevada. He traveled a lot, searching for unspoiled wilderness. He often visited Alaska. He became known as a travel writer and a philosopher who celebrated wilderness for its own sake.

Muir understood the interconnectedness of the natural world. As he would write of the Yosemite Valley, "the branching canyons and valleys of the basin of the streams that pour into Yosemite are as closely related as are the finger to the palm of the hand—as to branches, foliage, of a tree to the trunk." In Muir's view, human beings were part of an interconnected natural system. Natural wonders like Yosemite were, to Muir, places of deep spiritual meaning. They should be protected by their human visitors. In 1897, Muir wrote an article for the *Atlantic Monthly* magazine. He argued for a system of national parks to preserve America's remaining wilderness areas:

> *Any fool can destroy trees. They cannot run away; and if they could they would still be destroyed—chased and hunted down as long as fun or a dollar could be got out of their bark hides, branching horns, or magnificent bole backbones. Few that fell trees plant them; nor would planting avail much towards getting back anything like the noble primeval forests. During a man's life only saplings can be grown, in the place of the old trees—tens of centuries old—that have been destroyed. It took more than three thousand years to make some of the trees in these Western woods—trees that are still standing in perfect strength and beauty, waving and singing in the mighty forests of the Sierra. Through all the wonderful, eventful centuries since Christ's*

time—and long before that—God has cared for these trees, saved them from drought, disease, avalanches, and a thousand straining, leveling tempests and floods; but he cannot save them from fools—only Uncle Sam can do that.

GIFFORD PINCHOT

Muir and other conservationists felt that they had found an ally in Gifford Pinchot. Pinchot was America's first scientifically trained forester. Like Roosevelt, he came from a wealthy background. Also, like Roosevelt, he had pursued a totally unexpected career. Pinchot studied at the French Forest School. He believed in "scientific management" of forests. As Muir had noted in his 1897 *Atlantic Monthly* article, trees took a long time to grow. In the nineteenth century, timber companies treated forests as though they were fields of grain. The results of these clearcutting practices were bare hillsides, erosion, and flooding. It would be several generations before new trees grew up for harvesting. So the timber companies moved on to despoil still more wilderness. Pinchot

THE SIERRA CLUB

In 1892, John Muir helped found the Sierra Club. His goal was "to do something for wilderness and make the mountains glad." Muir served as the group's president until his death in 1914. The Sierra Club was devoted "to enlist the support and cooperation of the people and the government in preserving the forests and other natural features of the Sierra Nevada." It was also an outing club. Its members organized camping trips to the Sierra Nevada.

Over the years, the Sierra Club grew into an organization with a nationwide agenda of preservation. Its membership numbers also grew. The club had 27 original members. By the start of the twenty-first century, there were more than 450,000 members. The Sierra Club has 1.3 million members today. Other prominent conservationist organizations include the National Audubon Society, founded in 1905, the Wilderness Society, founded in 1935, and the Nature Conservancy, founded in 1951.

argued for government regulations of timber cutting. He hoped these would lead to "sustained yield." This meant that forests should be selectively pruned rather than cut down to the ground. These policies would be good for the environment. They would also be good for the long-term interests of the timber industry.

Muir had known Pinchot since 1893. The two men liked each other and went camping together. In 1898, Pinchot became chief of the Federal Forestry Division. (This group was reorganized in 1905 as the U.S. Forest Service, a bureau of the Department of Agriculture.) Teddy Roosevelt was another of Pinchot's friends. As president, Roosevelt wanted to adopt Pinchot's ideas to protect the wilderness.

But by that time Muir no longer considered Pinchot a reliable ally in the fight for preserving wilderness. Pinchot wanted to permit "multiple use" of America's forests. He allowed leasing public lands for logging and mining. These practices amounted to "multiple abuse" to Muir. Muir and Pinchot found themselves on opposite sides in a number of controversies. These included the decision to dam the river in Hetch Hetchy Valley, part of the Yosemite parkland. The dam was built. It was a bitter defeat for the Sierra Club and for Muir personally.

ROOSEVELT'S RECORD AS CONSERVATIONIST

Muir continued to regard Pinchot's boss, Teddy Roosevelt, as a friend of conservation. Roosevelt was not as strict a preservationist as Muir would have liked, but Roosevelt also was not sympathetic to those who had plundered the nation's public land resources. When Roosevelt stepped into the White House, Muir wrote to him. He gave Roosevelt advice on conservation policy. Roosevelt often acted on Muir's advice.

In 1891, Congress allowed the president to create forest reserve areas. This power went virtually unnoticed until Teddy Roosevelt became president. Within a few years, he had set aside 235 million acres (95 million ha) of land as forest reserves. These lands were administered by the Forest Service. Roosevelt created five new national parks. The Antiquities Act of 1906 allowed the creation of national monuments. Congress had intended these monuments to be historical sites, such as the remains of Native American villages in the Southwest. Roosevelt included scenic wonders. He made 800,000 acres (323,748 ha) along the Colorado River

In this 1906 photograph, Theodore Roosevelt (*left*) and John Muir stand on Glacier Point overlooking California's Yosemite Valley. Roosevelt, who often took Muir's advice, would later designate Muir Woods, 559 acres (226 ha) of redwood forest in Marin County, California, a national monument.

in Arizona the Grand Canyon National Monument in 1908. In 1920, the Grand Canyon became a national park. All told, Roosevelt created 16 national monuments. He also created 51 national wildlife refuges. The wildlife refuge was another innovation of his presidency.

Roosevelt and Muir finally met in 1903. Muir took Roosevelt on a three-day guided tour of the Yosemite Valley. They were joined only by their pack mules and a cook. The first night they slept under the stars in a grove of giant sequoias. Roosevelt later described the scene:

> *It was clear weather, and we lay in the open, the enormous cin-namon colored trunks rising above us like the columns of a vaster and more beautiful cathedral than was ever conceived by any human architect.*

On their second night out, they camped at Glacier Point on the southern rim of the valley. They cooked beefsteaks over an open fire. The president called the meal "bully," his favorite word of praise. The next morning they awoke to find that four inches of snow had fallen on them during the night. The president found this to be even "bullier yet!" Muir was impressed to find that Roosevelt knew so much natural history. Roosevelt could identify birds such as the western hermit thrush by their song. He scolded the president, however, for the delight he took in hunting. "When are you going to get beyond the boyishness of killing things?" Muir asked bluntly. The president was not offended. He also had no intention of giving up hunting.

MUIR AND ROOSEVELT'S LEGACY

All in all, Teddy Roosevelt had a great time on the trip and was grate-ful to Muir. In 1908, he would make Muir Woods, a northern Califor-nia redwood forest, a national monument. The year after Muir's death in 1914, Roosevelt wrote an obituary in which he described Muir as "a great factor in influencing the thought of California and the thought of the entire country so as to secure the preservation of those great natural phenomena—wonderful canyons, giant trees, slopes of flower-spangled hillsides—which make California a veritable Garden of the Lord." He ended: "Our generation owes much to John Muir."

Muir and Roosevelt both valued wilderness. For Muir, protect-ing the wilderness was a sacred trust. For Roosevelt, protecting the wilderness preserved the values of the "strenuous life." Muir was an idealist. Roosevelt was a practical politician. But for a few years at the dawn of the twentieth century, the two men accomplished more on behalf of the remaining American wilderness than anyone who came before them.

Chronology

1803	France sells the Louisiana Territory to the United States for $15 million, adding 828,000 square miles (1,332,536 square km) to the United States.
1804	William Dunbar and George Hunter, on an expedition to explore the southern tributaries of the Mississippi River, are the first Americans to bathe in the thermal hot springs of present-day Hot Springs, Arkansas.

Timeline

1803
France sells the Louisiana Territory to the United States for $15 million

1806–1807
Zebulon Pike maps most of the southern portion of the Louisiana Purchase

1803

1811

1804–1806
Lewis and Clark Expedition is successful in mapping the Missouri, Columbia, and Yellowstone rivers. They also find passages through the Rockies, establish first contact with western Native American tribes, and lay the basis for future U.S. claims on territory in the Pacific Northwest

1811
David Thompson crosses Athabasca Pass, which becomes the main fur trade route over the Rockies

1804–1806   Lewis and Clark Expedition fails to find a water route linking the Atlantic and Pacific oceans, but is successful in mapping the Missouri, Columbia, and Yellowstone rivers. They also find passages through the Rockies, establish first contact with Native American tribes in the West, and lay the basis for future U.S. claims on territory in the Pacific Northwest.

1805   The Freeman-Custis Expedition, on a mission to finish the work of the Dunbar-Hunter Expedition to explore the Mississippi's southern tributaries, reaches a spot on the Red River near present-day Texarkana but must turn back due to threats by the Spanish authorities.

1824
Jedediah Smith leads first party of U.S. citizens through South Pass from east to west

1867
William H. Seward agrees to pay the Russian-American Company $7.2 million for Alaska

1821

1867

1821
The Hudson's Bay Company and the North West Company merge. Their territory now covers 3 million square miles (4,828,032 square km) and the company has 1,500 employees

1843
John C. Frémont's report on his successful 1842 expedition to the Rockies makes him a popular hero and encourages wagonloads of emigrants to head west

◆ Zebulon Pike leads an expedition to find the headwaters of the Mississippi. He fails to do so but does purchase on behalf of the U.S. government more than 150,000 acres (60,702 hectares) of land from the Dakota Sioux. This was the first treaty signed between the U.S. government and a tribe west of the Mississippi.

1806–1807 On a mission to find the headwaters of the Red River, Zebulon Pike maps most of the southern portion of the Louisiana Purchase.

1809 David Thompson claims for Great Britain the region stretching from present-day northern Idaho to present-day Washington State. He opens up three new trading posts for the North West Company.

1811 David Thompson crosses Athabasca Pass, which becomes the main fur trade route over the Rockies.

1812 Wilson Price Hunt beats Lewis and Clark's travel time from St. Louis to the Pacific by two months.

1816 Congress establishes the Topographical Engineers Bureau, which plays a leading role in mapping the western United States.

1821 The Hudson's Bay Company and the North West Company merge. Their territory now covers 3 million square miles (4,828,032 square km) and the company has 1,500 employees.

1824 Jedediah Smith leads first party of U.S. citizens through South Pass from east to west. Later, thousands of settlers going to the West use this same route.

1827 Jedediah Smith crosses Ebbetts Pass and the Great Basin, reaching the Great Salt Lake on June 27. This was one of the most difficult journeys in North American exploration.

1843 John C. Frémont's report on his successful 1842 expedition to the Rockies makes him a popular hero and encourages wagonloads of emigrants to head west.

1846	Construction begins on the Smithsonian Institution in Washington, D.C., a towering brick castle with a museum, art gallery, library, lecture halls, and offices.
1867	U.S. Secretary of State William H. Seward agrees to pay the Russian-American Company $7.2 million for Alaska. Many Americans believe it is a waste of money, naming the territory Seward's Folly.
1869	On a three-month geographic expedition, John Wesley Powell and crew journey down the Green and Colorado rivers. They are the first to go down into the Grand Canyon.

Glossary

arid—Dry, with little moisture.

barometer—A scientific instrument for measuring atmospheric pressure.

botany—The branch of biology that studies plant life.

cache—A hiding place for provisions.

cartography—The design and production of maps.

chronometer—An especially accurate timekeeper used to determine longitude.

climate—Weather conditions of a region.

commerce—Trade and business; the interchange of goods.

confluence—A flowing together of two or more streams.

continental divide—High ground dividing river systems that flow into different oceans.

diplomacy—The conduct of negotiations and other relations between separate states or nations.

empire—A collection of nations or peoples ruled by a single powerful central government.

geology—The science that studies Earth's surface and subsurface and that seeks to understand the natural processes that have shaped both.

headwaters—The origin of a stream or river.

interpreter—Someone appointed to translate what is said in a foreign language.

keelboat—A shallow freight boat used for river travel; widely used on the Mississippi and Missouri rivers in the early nineteenth century.

latitude—The angular distance north or south from the equator of a point on Earth's surface, measured on the meridian of the point.

longitude—The angular distance east or west on Earth's surface, determined by the angle contained between the meridian of a particular place and the prime meridian, which runs through Greenwich, England.

meridian—A great imaginary circle of Earth that passes through the poles and any given point on Earth's surface.

missionary—A person sent to spread his or her religious faith to nonbelievers, often in another country.

musket—A smooth-bored, muzzle-loaded firearm, the standard infantry weapon of the eighteenth and early nineteenth century.

naturalist—A person engaged in the study of natural history, such as zoology and botany.

navigation—The art or science of directing the course of a ship.

pelts—Animal skins with the fur still attached.

pinnacle—The highest or culminating point.

plateau—A raised landform with a level surface.

portage—The act of carrying boats or goods from one navigable body of water to another or the place where such things can be carried.

primeval—Having to do with very early ages in Earth's history.

scurvy—A potentially fatal disease caused by diets lacking in fruits and vegetables, leading to vitamin C deficiency and marked by bleeding gums.

specimen—A typical animal, plant, mineral, or part taken in a scientific sample and considered to exemplify a whole mass or number.

topography—The detailed description and analysis of the features of a relatively small area, district, or locality.

tributary—A stream contributing its flow to a larger stream or body of water.

zoology—The branch of the biological sciences that concerns the study of animals.

Bibliography

Allen, John Logan, ed. *North American Exploration.* 3 vols. Lincoln: University of Nebraska Press, 1997.

Axtell, James. *Beyond 1492: Encounters in Colonial North America.* New York: Oxford University Press, 1992.

Benson, Maxine. *From Pittsburgh to the Rocky Mountains: Major Stephen Long's Expedition, 1819–1820.* Golden, Colo.: Fulcrum, 1988.

Chaffin, Tom. *Pathfinder: John Charles Frémont and the Course of American Empire.* New York: Hill and Wang, 2002.

Debo, Angie. *A History of the Indians of the United States.* Norman: University of Oklahoma Press, 1984.

Dickason, Olive P. *Canada's First Nations: A History of Founding Peoples from Earliest Times.* Norman: University of Oklahoma Press, 1992.

Foley, William E., and C. David Rice. *The First Chouteaus: River Barons of Early St. Louis.* Urbana: University of Illinois Press, 1983.

Haycox, Stephen. *Alaska: An American Colony.* Seattle: University of Washington Press, 2002.

Lamar, Howard R., ed. *The New Encyclopedia of the American West.* New Haven: Yale University Press, 1998.

MacFarlane, Robert. *Mountains of the Mind.* New York: Pantheon Books, 2003.

Milner, Clyde A., et al., eds. *The Oxford History of the American West.* New York: Oxford University Press, 1994.

Moore, Terris. *Mount McKinley: The Pioneer Climbs.* Seattle, Wash.: The Mountaineers, 1981.

Ronda, James P. *Astoria and Empire.* Lincoln: University of Nebraska Press, 1990.

Schwantee, Carlos, ed. *Encounters with a Distant Land: Exploration and the Great Northwest.* Moscow: University of Idaho Press, 1994.

Schwartz, Seymour I. *The Mismapping of America.* Rochester, N.Y.: University of Rochester Press, 1993.

Streshinsky, Shirley. *Audubon: Life and Art in the American Wilderness.* New York: Villard Books, 1993.

Stuart, Reginald C. *United States Expansion and British North America, 1775–1871.* Charlotte: University of North Carolina Press, 1988.

Udall, Stewart L. *The Forgotten Founders: Rethinking the History of the Old West.* Washington, D.C.: Island Press, 2002.

Utley, Robert M. *A Life Wild and Perilous: Mountain Men and the Paths to the Pacific*. New York: Henry Holt, 1997.

Viola, Herman J. *Exploring the West*. Washington, D.C.: Smithsonian Press, 1987.

Waldman, Carl, Alan Wexler, and Jon Cunningham. *Encyclopedia of Exploration*. New York: Facts On File, 2004.

Wilkins, Thurman. *John Muir: Apostle of Nature*. Norman: University of Oklahoma Press, 1995.

Williams, Glyn. *Voyages of Delusion: The Quest for the Northwest Passage*. New Haven, Conn.: Yale University Press, 2002.

Further Resources

Goetzmann, William H., et al. *Karl Bodmer's America.* Lincoln: University of Nebraska Press, 1984.

Greene, John C. *American Science in the Age of Jefferson.* Ames: Iowa State University Press, 1984.

Hughes, Robert. *American Visions: The Epic History of Art in America.* New York: Alfred A. Knopf, 1997.

Josephy, Alvin M., Jr. *500 Nations: An Illustrated History of North American Indians.* New York: Knopf, 1994.

Sellers, Charles Coleman. *Mr. Peale's Museum: Charles Willson Peale and the First Popular Museum of Natural Science and Art.* New York: W.W. Norton and Company, 1980.

Trenton, Patricia, and Peter H. Hassrick. *The Rocky Mountains: A Vision for Artists in the Nineteenth Century.* Norman: University of Oklahoma Press, 1983.

Wilson, James. *The Earth Shall Weep: A History of Native America.* New York: Atlantic Monthly Press, 1999.

FICTION

Gregory, Kristiana. *Dear America: Across the Wide and Lonesome Prairie: The Oregon Trail Diary of Hattie Campbell, 1847.* New York: Scholastic, 2003.

London, Jack. *The Call of the Wild.* Englewood Cliffs, N.J.: Prentice-Hall, 1990.

McCarthy, Gary. *Yosemite.* Chicago: Pinnacle Books, 1995.

McMurtry, Larry. *Sin Killer.* New York: Simon and Schuster, 2003.

Myers, Laurie. *Lewis and Clark and Me: A Dog's Tale.* New York: Henry Holt and Company, 2002.

WEB SITES

A Biography of America: Gallery of Peale Paintings
http://www.learner.org/biographyofamerica/prog03/feature/gallery_08.html
The companion Web site to the video series A Biography of America. *Includes biographies and image galleries.*

John Wesley Powell Memorial Museum
http://www.powellmuseum.org/MajorPowell.html
The biography of explorer John Wesley Powell and information about his expeditions. The site includes photographs, planning guides, and maps.

Lest We Forget: Beyond the Pale: African Americans in the Fur Trade West
http://www.coax.net/people/lwf/FURTRADE.HTM
A detailed history of the contributions of African Americans in the fur trade.

Mountain Man Plains Indian Canadian Fur Trade
http://www.thefurtrapper.com/
The Web site for collecting and sharing information on the Rocky Mountain fur trade between the mountain men and the Plains Indians.

Nebraskastudies.org: Fur Traders and Missionaries
http://www.nebraskastudies.org/0400/frameset_reset.html
Detailed information about western exploration, including information about the Louisiana Purchase, fur traders like Manuel Lisa, and forts. Includes teacher activities and multimedia.

PBS: Harriman Expedition Retraced: A Century of Change
http://www.pbs.org/harriman/index.html
The online book about Edward Harriman's expedition to Alaska. Includes maps, charts, photographs, and biographical information.

PBS: New Perspectives on the West: Kit Carson
http://www.pbs.org/weta/thewest/people/a_c/carson.htm
The Public Broadcasting System's online source for information about explorers of the West, including Kit Carson, a key figure of the United States' westward expansion.

Smithsonian American Art Museum: Campfire Stories with George Catlin
http://catlinclassroom.si.edu/cl.html
This Web site has hundreds of George Catlin's artworks, plus historical documents and commentary from historians.

Picture Credits

Index

A

African Americans, 56, 108
agriculture, 14, 71, 90
Alarcón, Hernando de, 10
Alaska
    American explorers and, 118–124
    early exploration of, 114–115
    fur trade and traders, 46
    Russia and, 115–118
Aleut people, 115
Allen, Henry Tureman, 121
American Fur Company, 48
Anasazi Indians, 17
annexation, of California, 94–97
Arctic Circle, 114
Arikara Indians, 51
Arkansas River, 37
artists
    landscape artists, 105–106
    Long expedition and, 74, 77
    Native Americans and, 101–105
    photography, 106
    western nostalgia and, 107–108
Ashley, William H., 13, 21, 55–56
Aster, John Jacob, 47–53, 67
Athabasca region, 62–63
Atkinson, Henry W., 74, 75
Audubon, John James, 104

B

Baranov, Aleksandr, 117
Bear Flag Rebellion, 95
beavers, 58
    See also fur trade and traders
Beckwourth, Jim, 56
Benton, Thomas Hart, 79, 80, 84, 87
Bering, Vitus, 115–116
Bierstadt, Albert, 105
Big Horn River, 46
Birds of America, The (Audubon), 104
Black Hills, 81, 83
Blackfeet Indians, 47
Blue Water Creek, Battle of, 81

boats
    first Pike expedition and, 32
    John C. Frémont and, 87
    John Jacob Aster and, 48
    Long expedition and, 74–75
    Powell expedition and, 11, 13–14, 16–17
    second Pike expedition and, 37
Bodmer, Karl, 103, 105
Bonneville, Benjamin Louis Eulalie de, 58
borders, of Canada, 68
Bradley, George Young, 11, 16, 18
British settlers, 30, 53, 62
British territory, Hudson's Bay Company and, 67–68
Brooks, Alfred Hulse, 121
Brown, Baptiste, 13
buffalo, 103, 128
Burr, Aaron, 31, 35, 40

C

Cabrillo, Juan Rodríguez, 85
Calhoun, James C., 75
California
    exploration of, 84–87
    Jedediah Smith and, 57
    John C. Frémont and, 87–90, 91–94, 97–98
    John Muir and, 133
    U.S. annexation of, 94–97
Call of the Wild, The (London), 123
Canada, western
    Alexander Mackenzie and, 64
    Canadian nationalism and, 68–71
    David Thompson and, 65–67
    exploration of, 59–60
    Hudson's Bay Company and, 60–62, 67–68
    North West Company, 62–63
Canadian Pacific Railway, 70
Canadian River, 76–77
Cárdenas, García López de, 10
Carson, Kit, 87, 90, 94
Cartier, Jacques, 43, 59

Cataract Canyon, 16–17
Catlin, George, 102–103
Cavelier, René-Robert (La Salle), 60
Champlain, Samuel de, 43, 59–60
Chirikov, Alexei, 115–116
Chouteau, Auguste-Pierre, 46–47
Chouteau family, 45–46, 46–47
Chronology, 134–137
Civil War, the, 83, 98, 109
Clark, William, 8, 23, 102
Clatsop Indians, 52
climate, 89, 92, 114
Colorado River, 9–11, 110
Colter, John, 46–47
Columbia River, 48, 50, 52, 65–66, 67, 68
conservation issues. See wilderness
    preservation
Coronado, Francisco Vásquez de, 30
cowboys, 107–108
Custis, Peter, 29

D
Dakota Sioux Indians, 32–33
Dall, William Healey, 119–120, 122
Dana, Henry Richard, 86
Dominguez, Anastasio, 17, 21
Donner Pass, 92
Drake, Francis, 85–86
Dunbar, William, 23, 26–29
Dunbar-Hunter expedition, 26–29
Dunn, Bill, 11, 19, 21

E
economic development, 78, 97
Emory, William H., 80–81
English explorers
    California and, 85–86
    exploring western Canada and,
        60–62
    fur trade and traders, 44–45
Erie Canal, 82
Eriksson, Leif, 59
Escalante River, 112
Escalante, Silvestre Vélez de., 17, 21

F
Fedorov, Ivan, 115
Ferrelo, Bartolomé, 85
Florez, Manuel Antonio, 30
food and supplies
    first Pike expedition and, 33–34
    Long expedition and, 75

Powell expedition and, 7–8, 11, 14
    second Pike expedition and, 37
forest reserves, 131
forestry, Gifford Pinchot and, 130–131
Fort Astoria, 50, 52, 67
Fort George, 53
Fort Raymond, 46
Fort Ross, 117
Fort Yukon, 120
fossils, 100, 101
Freeman, Thomas, 29
Freeman-Custis expedition, 28, 29–31
free-trading system, fur trade and,
    55–56
Frémont, John C., 13, 21, 82
    first California expedition, 87–90
    legacy of, 98–99
    second California expedition, 91–94
    third California expedition, 97–98
    U.S. annexation of California and,
        94–97
    U.S. Army Corps of Topographical
        Engineers and, 78–80
French and Indian War, 45, 62
French explorers, 43, 59–60
Fulton, Robert, 82
fur trade and traders
    Alaska and, 115, 116–117
    California and, 86
    Chouteau family and, 45–46
    decline of, 58
    exploring western Canada and,
        68–69
    first Pike expedition and, 34
    Hudson's Bay Company and, 61
    Jedediah Smith and, 56–58
    John Jacob Aster and, 47–53
    Manuel Lisa, 46–47
    North West Company and, 62–63
    origins of the fur trade, 42–45
    Snake River expeditions and, 54–55
    War of 1812 and, 53–54
    William H. Ashley and, 55–56

G
geologists, 108–113
Gettysburg, Battle of, 83
Gillespie, Archibald, 94–95
gold, discovery of, 83, 84, 97–98, 124
Goodman, Frank, 11, 13, 14, 16
government, of Canada, 69

Grand Canyon, the, 20
    the Colorado River and, 9–11
    national parks and monuments,
      132
    photography and, 113
    Powell expedition and, 7–9, 11–14,
      16–19, 21, 110, 111
    Thomas Moran and, 106
Great American Desert, 40, 77–78
Great Basin, the, 88
Great Lakes, the, 59–60
Great Salt Lake, 87–88, 92
Great Valley, California, 90
Green River, 10, 15
Gvozdev, Mikhail, 115

H ————
habitat destruction, westward
    expansion and, 125
Harriman, Edward Henry, 122–123
Harris, Moses, 56
Hime, Humphrey Lloyd, 106
Hind, Henry Youle, 106
Hopi Indians, 17
hot springs, 27
Howland, Oramel, 11, 13, 14, 19, 21
Howland, Seneca, 11, 13, 14, 19, 21
Hudson Bay, 60–61
Hudson's Bay Company
    Alaska and, 120
    David Thompson and, 65
    exploring western Canada and,
      60–62, 67–68
    North West Company and, 67–68
    Oregon Territory and, 54
    Peter Skene Ogden and, 54–55
Hunt, Wilson Price, 50–53
Hunter, George, 27–29
hunting, 128, 133

I ————
ice age, Alaska and, 114–115
Inuit people, 115, 116
Irving, Washington, 50, 58
Ives, Joseph Christmas, 81, 83, 106

J ————
James, Edwin, 75, 76, 77
Jefferson, Thomas
    Alexander Mackenzie and, 66
    Dunbar-Hunter expedition, 26–29
    fossils and, 101

    Freeman-Custis expedition, 28,
      29–31
    John Jacob Aster and, 48
    Lewis and Clark expedition, 22–23
    Louisiana Purchase and, 23–26
    Zebulon Pike and, 31–41
Jolliet, Louis, 60

K ————
Kearny, Stephen Watts, 96, 97
Kennerman, Henry, 34, 36
Kennicott, Robert, 118, 119
King, Charles Bird, 101–102

L ————
landscape artists, 105–106
Lee, Robert E., 80
Lewis and Clark expedition, 22–23, 25,
    46, 50–51, 65, 66
Lewis, Meriwether, 8, 22, 23, 46
Lisa, Manuel, 46–47
Livingston, Robert, 25
London, Jack, 123
Long expedition, 73–78
Long, Stephen Harriman, 73–74, 83
Long's Peak, 76
Louisiana Purchase, 23–26

M ————
Macdonald, John Alexander, 69–70
Mackenzie, Alexander, 62, 63, 64
Mandan Indians, 103
maps
    Alaska and, 117, 120
    Alexander Mackenzie and, 63
    David Thompson and, 65
    Dunbar-Hunter expedition and, 27
    exploring western Canada and, 70
    Hunt expedition and, 52
    John C. Frémont and, 79, 90
    John Wesley Powell and, 112–113
    Louisiana Purchase and, 28
    second Pike expedition and, 39
    third Frémont expedition, 91
    U.S. Army Corps of Topographical
      Engineers and, 72, 80–81
Marquette, Jacques, 60
Maximilian, Prince, 103, 105
Mexican American War, 80–81
Mexico, 86–87, 93–94
military explorers, Alaska and, 120–121
Mississippi River, 31–32, 79, 81

Missouri River, 26–27, 74
modern life, Alaska and, 124
Mojave Desert, 57
Monroe, James, 25
Moran, Thomas, 105–106
mountain men, 42, 55–56
mountaineering, Alaska and, 122
Muir, John, 121–122, 122–123, 129–130, 131, 132–133
museums, 100, 101

N

national parks and monuments, 103, 129–130, 131–132
nationalism, Canadian, 68–71
Native Americans
    Alaska and, 114, 115, 123–124
    artists and, 101–105
    Colorado River and, 10
    fur trade and traders, 55
    Jedediah Smith and, 58
    John C. Frémont and, 89, 94
    Lewis and Clark expedition and, 23
    Louisiana Purchase and, 27
    Powell expedition and, 14, 17, 19, 21
    reservations and, 125
    trade networks and, 42–43
    U.S. Army Corps of Topographical Engineers and, 81, 83
    Zebulon Pike and, 32, 35, 36
    See also specific tribes
natural history, 100–101, 104, 108, 109, 118–119, 126
Nez Perce Indians, 23
Nicollet, Joseph N., 79
Nolan, Philip, 25–26
Norse explorers, 59
North West Company, 46, 53–54, 62–63, 65, 67–68
Northwest Passage, 22, 23, 60

O

Ogden, Peter Skene, 54–55
Oñate, Juan de, 30
Oregon Territory, 48, 53, 67, 68, 80, 87
Osage Indians, 36
Otoe Indians, 76

P

Pacific Fur Company, 48, 50
Pacific Northwest. *See* Oregon Territory
Paiute Indians, 19, 21

Pawnee Indians, 36, 37, 75
Peale, Charles Willson, 100, 101
Peale, Titian Ramsey, 74, 77
personnel
    Freeman-Custis expedition, 29
    Long expedition, 74, 75
    Powell expedition, 11, 17–18
    second Pike expedition, 36, 38
    third Frémont expedition, 92
photography, 106, 113
Pike, Zebulon Montgomery, 31–41
Pike's Peak, 37, 41, 76
Pinchot, Gifford, 130–131
Platte River, 75–76
Polk, James K., 68, 91–92, 97
population, of Alaska, 123–124
Powell expedition
    beginning of, 11–13
    Colorado River and, 110
    difficulties of, 13–14, 15–19
    the Grand Canyon and, 7–9
    separation of party and, 19
Powell, John Wesley, 7, 8, 11, 12, 16, 18, 108–113

R

railroads, 78, 81, 82
Ranne, Peter, 56
rapids, Powell expedition and, 13–14, 18–19
Raymond, Charles, 120
Real Alencaster, Joaquin del, 38–39
Red River, 26–27, 29, 35, 38
Remington, Frederic, 108
reputation
    John C. Frémont and, 90, 97, 98–99
    John Wesley Powell and, 110, 113
    Zebulon Pike and, 40, 41
Robinson, John H., 36, 38
rock climbing, 12, 16
Rocky Mountain Fur Company, 55
Rocky Mountains
    Albert Bierstadt and, 105
    Alexander Mackenzie and, 63, 66
    Benjamin Louis Eulalie de Bonneville and, 58
    Colorado River and, 9–10
    David Thompson and, 65–66, 67
    fur trade and traders, 55–56
    John C. Frémont and, 79–80, 97
    John Wesley Powell and, 110

Lewis and Clark expedition and, 22
Long expedition and, 75
second Pike expedition and, 37
Transcontinental Railroad and, 82
Roosevelt, Theodore, 125–128, 131–133
Russell, Andrew J., 106
Russia, Alaska and, 115–118
Russian American Company, 46, 117

S

Salish Indians, 50
San Francisco Bay, 93
San Gabriel River, Battle of, 96
Sangre de Cristo Mountains, 38
Schwatka, Frederick, 120
scientific expeditions
    Alaska and, 118–120, 121–122
    John Wesley Powell and, 108–113,
        111–113
    Long expedition and, 74, 76–77
    natural history collections, 100–101
    Powell expedition and, 8, 17–18
settlers
    California and, 94, 95
    exploring western Canada and, 69,
        71
Seward, William H., 118
Seymour, Samuel, 74, 77
Shelikhov, Grigorii, 117
Shoshone Indians, 23
Sibley, John, 23, 29
Sierra Club, 130
Sierra Nevada Mountains, 57–58, 88–
    90, 92–93, 129
Sioux Indians, 81, 83
Sloat, John Drake, 95, 96
Smith, Jedediah, 56, 56–58, 86
Smithson, James, 101
Smithsonian Institution, the, 101
Snake River, 51, 54–55
Southwest, American, 30
Spanish explorers, 10, 30, 85
Spanish territory
    California and, 84, 86
    Freeman-Custis expedition, 29–30
    Jedediah Smith and, 57
    Russia and, 117
    St. Louis and, 46
    Zebulon Pike and, 35–36, 38–40
Spanish-American War, 128
St. Lawrence River, 59, 60

St. Louis fur trade, 46–47
St. Louis Missouri Fur Company, 46, 47
statehood, California and, 98
steamboats, 74–75, 82
Stockton, Robert F., 96
"Strenuous Life, The" (Roosevelt), 128
Sumner, Jack, 11, 110
supplies. See food and supplies
Sutter, John, 86, 94, 117

T

Talleyrand-Périgord, Charles-Maurice
    de, 25
Taylor, Zachary, 94
telegraph lines, 118–119
Teton Mountains, 46
Texas, 25–26
Thompson, Almon Harris, 111, 112
Thompson, David, 65–67
Thorn, Jonathan, 48, 50
timber industry, 130–131
tourism, Alaska and, 122–123
trading posts. See fur trade and traders
Transcontinental Railroad, 82, 98, 106,
    107
treaties, with Native Americans, 32–33
Treaty of 1818, 53
Treaty of Guadalupe Hidalgo, 80
Two Years Before the Mast (Dana), 86

U

Ulloa, Francisco de, 10
U.S. Army Corps of Topographical
    Engineers, 72
    John C. Frémont and, 78–80
    Long expedition and, 73–78
    Mexican American War and, 80–81
    Native Americans and, 81, 83
    Transcontinental Railroad and, 82
U.S. Forest Service, 131
U.S. Geological Survey (USGS), 113,
    121
U.S. Mexico Boundary Commission,
    80–81
Ute Indians, 14

V

Vancouver, George, 63

W

War of 1812, 40–41, 53–54, 69
Warren, Gouverneur Kemble, 81, 83
western nostalgia, art and, 107–108

westward expansion
  American Southwest and, 30
  California and, 84
  habitat destruction and, 125
  John C. Frémont and, 79, 91–92
  Mexican American War and, 80
  Thomas Jefferson and, 23–25
  Transcontinental Railroad and, 82
  U.S. Army Corps of Topographical
    Engineers and, 78
"Wild West," the, 107–108
wilderness preservation
  Gifford Pinchot and, 130–131
  John Muir and, 129–130

the Sierra Club and, 130
Theodore Roosevelt and, 125–128,
  131–133
Wilkinson, James, 31, 35, 39–40
Wilkinson, James Biddle (son), 36, 36–37
Wind River Mountains, 57

Y

Yellowstone expedition, 74, 75
Yellowstone National Park, 103
Yellowstone River, 46
York (slave), 56
Yosemite Valley, 129, 132–133
Yukon River, 120

About the Contributors

Author and general editor **MAURICE ISSERMAN** holds a B.A. in history from Reed College and an M.A. and Ph.D. in history from the University of Rochester. He is a professor of history at Hamilton College, specializing in twentieth-century U.S. history and the history of exploration. Isserman was a Fulbright distinguished lecturer at Moscow State University. He is the author of 12 books.

General editor **JOHN S. BOWMAN** received a B.A. in English literature from Harvard University and matriculated at Trinity College, Cambridge University, as Harvard's Fiske Scholar and at the University of Munich. Bowman has worked as an editor and as a freelance writer for more than 40 years. He has edited numerous works of history, as well as served as general editor of Chelsea House's AMERICA AT WAR set. Bowman is the author of more than 10 books, including a volume in this series, *Exploration in the World of the Ancients, Revised Edition*.